T0208018

Warpaint

Raising a generation of daughters
to know their worth in Christ Jesus,
encouraging them to embrace their uniqueness,
and empowering them with the Word of
God to fight the good fight.

STEPHANIE ARCENEAUX

WESTBOW
PRESS®
A DIVISION OF THOMAS NELSON
& ZONDERVAN

WestBow Press books may be ordered through booksellers or by contacting:

WestBow Press
A Division of Thomas Nelson & Zondervan
1663 Liberty Drive
Bloomington, IN 47403
www.westbowpress.com
844-714-3454

ISBN: 978-1-6642-7427-3 (sc)
ISBN: 978-1-6642-7428-0 (hc)
ISBN: 978-1-6642-7426-6 (e)

Library of Congress Control Number: 2022914045

Print information available on the last page.

WestBow Press rev. date: 10/12/2022

CONTENTS

DEDICATION

I dedicate this book to my daughters, Sarah Ashton and Sophie Annabelle. You are my miracle babies and my greatest gift. You have filled my heart and my life with love and joy. I'm so thankful and amazed that God chose me to be your mother. This book is my legacy that I leave to you.

Lord, I will worship you with extended hands as my
whole heart explodes with praise! I will tell everyone
everywhere about your wonderful works and how
your marvelous miracles exceed expectations.

Psalm 9:1 (TPT)

INTRODUCTION

Raising a generation of daughters to know their worth in Christ Jesus, encouraging them to embrace and celebrate their uniqueness, and empowering them with the Word of God to fight the good fight.

This is not a "how to" book. I am in no way an expert in child rearing practices. I didn't even become a parent until I was forty-two years old. Since I was older when I had my girls, I believed that I should have been wiser about parenting, but I experienced parenthood like everyone else, you learn as you go. You make mistakes along the way, and pray that you haven't scarred your children for life.

For the past nine years, I've watched my identical twin daughters, Sarah and Sophie, grow from these teeny tiny premature babies into these beautiful, smart, creative, tall, skinny mini-mes; each one possessing their own combination of my personality traits. As a mother, I want the best for my daughters, but when I look at the world in which we live today, I have pause for concern about the struggles and difficulties facing them as they grow older.

This world can be a scary place for our innocent little girls. As a mother, I want to protect my daughters from the pains, the harsh realities, and any kind of mistreatment. The world has dramatically changed since I was a child; it seems more mixed-up than ever.

The world's influences on our daughters come in many forms; the traditional forms are the television shows they watch and the advertisements they see, the music they listen to, books and magazines they read, and the friends and peers they spend time with. However, today the biggest influence on our children is social media which I see as a blessing and a curse, simultaneously. All of these sources are bombarding our children with one message: who the world says they should be.

The world tells our daughters what they should look like, what type of clothing they should wear, how they should style their hair and makeup, what kind of handbag they should carry, and what kind of car they should drive. The world says that you are only worthy, accepted, or important if you follow these trends. These are some of the more superficial forms of self-worth that the world promotes.

The world will try and tell our daughters what to believe about religion, politics, relationships, marriage, vocation, and gender. But as a mother and a Christian, I believe that it is my responsibility to make sure that my daughters' identities and self-worth are solely based on the truth of God's Word and who He says they are. I am not leaving that job to anyone else.

The world's opinions and ideologies change like the wind and shifting sand, but the Word of God does not change and therefore creates a solid foundation for my daughters and their lives. This is of significant importance to me because I believe that our parenting should be purpose driven and intentional. God has gifted me with these two precious souls that I must nurture, guide, and encourage along their journey. In my book, *Wait Is a Four-Letter Word*, I reference the scripture in James 1:17 (NIV) "Every good and perfect gift is from above, coming down from the Father of the heavenly lights, who does not change like shifting shadows," because my daughters were miracle babies whom I prayed for, for 10 years. Receiving such an amazing gift from God only strengthened my resolve to "bring [them] up in the nurture and admonition of the Lord" Ephesians 6:4 (KJV).

I know that "God is not a god of confusion but of peace" I Corinthians 14:33 (ESV). However, what I see in our world today is utter chaos and confusion. So many young women seem lost, adrift on the uncertain seas of life, and confused about who they are and what their purpose is. This continual aimless wandering must surely feel lonely and often tragically hopeless.

I dare say it, but it is the truth; we are living in an era of history more than ever when *right seems wrong and wrong seems right.*

I want more for my daughters than what the world has to offer them. I want what God has for them; an amazing life, an exciting journey, hundreds of promises to fill their lives with joy and steadfast hope. I want them to know that they are unique, and that God has called them for a specific purpose on this earth, an inconceivable plan that when fulfilled, will literally leave them speechless.

I know the dreams I have for my daughters sound quite lofty, and maybe even unrealistic or unattainable. I also realize that Sarah and Sophie have to be willing participants in these dreams. But God has birthed this dream inside me, and I know, that I know, that I know, when God has a plan for your daughters' lives, you can be 100% certain He will bring it to pass.

> Indeed I have spoken it; I will also bring it to pass. I have purposed it; I will also do it. Isaiah 46:11 (NKJV)

> Being confident of this, that he who began a good work in you will carry it on to completion until the day of Christ Jesus. Philippians 1:6 (NIV)

THE TITLE

Growing up I was always the tall, skinny, lanky, and awkward kid. I was always the tallest, or one of the tallest girls in my class. I was always taller than many of the boys, and I *always* had to stand in the back row with the boys for our school class picture. I was teased and made fun of sometimes, which of course, hurt my feelings. One time this *mean girl* called me Big Bird, obviously because I had really long, skinny, legs. When I told my mom about the name calling, she always said the *mean girl* was probably jealous of me, so I shouldn't let it bother me. I tried not to let the name calling bother me, but in reality, those words hurt.

I thought I had a fairly good self-esteem growing up. My parents always encouraged my brothers and I to do our best, whether it was: schoolwork, athletics, band, or any activity that we were involved in. I took ballet, tap, and twirling when I was little, but because my mom would wake me up from my nap to take me to dance, I would cry and complain that I didn't want to go. I really loved my naps back then and I still love my naps now, so napping took precedence over any other activities. After several weeks of whining and crying on the way to dance class, my mom just gave up and let me quit. When I got to middle school, I resumed twirling lessons because I wanted to try out for the eighth-grade twirling squad. My priorities had changed; napping was no longer important but being popular was. Making twirler meant that I would get to wear cute twirling uniforms, perform at Thursday afternoon pep rallies, and march with the marching band at Thursday night football games. I went from an obscure "nobody" to a popular "somebody." My identity began to take form and my self-esteem got a huge boost.

I was also in all honors classes and made excellent grades. I was in the National Honor Society; however, I didn't think it was such a big deal because school was easy for me, so I took accolades like NHS induction, for granted. I was always dedicated to doing my homework, studying for all my tests, and achieving above and beyond my grade level.

When I got to high school, the pressure began to mount because the stakes were even higher to be popular. My goal was to become an officer on the drill team; I made the drill team my sophomore year and lieutenant my senior year. I felt special because fourteen girls tried out for five positions, and I happen to be one of those five lucky girls chosen. I wasn't the world's best dancer, high kicker, or choreographer, but I must have impressed the band director and other judges because I was chosen to be a lieutenant.

One of my absolute best friends growing up was Amy; she and I met at the end of seventh grade when we both tried out for the eighth-grade twirling squad. I thought I was the best twirler and should be chosen as the head twirler, but the judges chose Amy instead. It was only a momentary disappointment, and we soon became great friends.

Amy's mom, Sue Ann, was a professional runway model; she was 5'11" and her looks were striking. She was very thin with flawless porcelain skin and jet-black hair cut into a chic jaw-length bob. She never wore a lot of makeup, but she always wore her signature blood-red lipstick. She walked the catwalk for hair shows, modeled clothing for local boutiques, and even made a commercial in Mexico City, Mexico.

She was graceful and quirky, all at the same time, and I was an instant admirer.

During our freshman year of high school Amy's mom opened Ultra Image, a modeling school. I was extremely excited because I had lofty aspirations of becoming a model one day, so my dad paid for six months of modeling classes. During each class we would learn various aspects of the modeling business; how to walk the runway in four-inch heels, how to apply stage makeup, and how to coordinate a wardrobe. I even had a professional photographer take some headshots of me, a gawky ninth grader with shiny silver braces. Not exactly what one would envision a model looking like, but I loved every minute of it.

Our first session was makeup application; Sue Ann demonstrated specific techniques used to apply makeup. She began by applying an ivory-colored liquid foundation to even out my skin tone, cover up the dark circles under my eyes, and any zits that I had, making sure my skin was smooth. Then she dusted my entire face with loose face powder. She told us that the skin on our face was like a blank canvas.

A painter begins with a flawless smooth linen canvas onto which he applies the colors that he has chosen to create his masterpiece. She explained that the analogy was the same with the skin on our face; you must start with a flawless canvas before using color to accentuate the rest of your features which includes your lips, eyes, and cheeks. She chose to paint my lips a shocking red which I absolutely loved. Up until that time, I wore subtle colors like pale pink, but all it took was one application of shocking red and I was hooked. It became my signature color and still is today.

The complete makeover was time-consuming, taking about an hour, but when she was done I stared into the mirror somewhat surprised and pleasantly pleased with the results. I looked different and older than a fifteen- year-old. When my mom picked me up from modeling school that evening, she was taken aback by the shocking red lipstick and heavy black eyeliner. She said that she couldn't wait for my dad to see me.

When we got home, I proudly walked into the living room where my dad was watching TV and said, "Well, what do you think?" *Shocked* is how I would describe the look on his face. He said, "Sister, you look like you're thirty-five years old! What happened to my little girl?" After that night I continued to wear the shocking red lipstick daily, but toned down the rest of the makeup. It became a joke between my dad and I; every time I would dress up to go out with my friends, he would say to me as I was coming down the staircase, "Looks like you've got your *warpaint* on," hence the title of this book.

WHAT IS BEAUTY?

But the Lord said unto Samuel, "Do not look at his appearance or at his physical stature, because I have refused him; for the Lord does not see as man sees; for man looks at the outward appearance, but the Lord looks at the heart." I Samuel 16: 7 (NKJV)

I can't remember a day while I was growing up when my mom didn't have on makeup. She called it, "Putting on her face." She put on her face every single day no matter what she had to do: chores around the house, running errands, grocery shopping, mowing the grass, going to weekly Bible study, or Sunday morning church service.

My mom is not a vain person. I believe she wore makeup to present her best self to others: she put on makeup, fixed her hair, and got dressed every day. She never wore yoga pants and a t-shirt, messy-hair-bun, and bare faced. Flip flops, yes, bare faced, NEVER! She wanted to present her best self to others every single day. She unconsciously communicated to me the importance of appearance, but not for vanity's sake. Putting yourself together each day was part of a daily routine. You put your best face forward ready to conquer the world, whatever that day may bring.

I began wearing makeup in middle school. My mom bought me lip gloss and eyeshadow, nothing else. She chose inconspicuous pale pink for my lips and light blue eyeshadow for my eyes. Colors that were barely noticeable on my pasty white skin, but colors that were on trend. Looking back now, I would never wear blue eye shadow with my blue eyes, but at the time I thought I looked good and that was all that mattered.

I didn't begin making up my entire face with foundation, powder, lipstick, blush, eye shadow, eyeliner and mascara until I attended modeling school during my freshman year of high school. The only reason I thought I would succeed as a model was because of my stature, tall and lanky, not because of my beauty. I was grateful Sue Ann taught me the proper techniques of makeup application, so I had the confidence when I left the house each day for school, I would look attractive, not like a circus clown.

Before we tackle three of the defining features of our visage, let's take a look at the definition of beauty. What is beauty and who defines what is beautiful? Webster's dictionary defines beauty as the quality or aggregate of qualities in a person or thing that gives pleasure to the senses, or pleasurably exalts the mind or spirit. What attributes decide whether a woman is beautiful or not? Flawless skin; ebony, ivory, freckles, or somewhere in between? Large almond shaped eyes, or small narrow eyes? Blue, black, brown eyes, or rare colors like green, hazel, or gray? High cheekbones or dimples? A round, oval, square or heart-shaped face? Blonde, brunette, black, or flaming red hair? This list could go on and on because there are countless combinations of facial attributes that are used to describe women and their beauty.

Who or what decides whether a woman is beautiful or not? Is

it oneself, your parents, your friends, *Vogue, Marie Claire, Seventeen* magazine, television, or social media? In all honesty, beauty is truly in the eye of the beholder; it is subjective not objective. Thank the good Lord above that He is our Beholder; the One who sees us and our unique beauty. The world's standards of beauty are in stark contrast to God's standards of beauty.

The Bible mentions several women who were considered great beauties: Sarah, Rebekah, Rachel, Bathsheba, Esther, Abishag the Shunammite woman, and Ruth, to name a few. But other women mentioned in the Bible held just as much beauty because they spent time in Jesus' presence serving Him. For example, Mary and Martha, the unnamed women with the alabaster jar washing His feet with expensive perfume, and accepting from Him the *living water* as the Samaritan woman did at the well.

All this talk about beauty may seem superficial; however, I believe God created our unique physical characteristics not just for practical purposes, i.e., lips to speak, eyes to see, and cheeks to smile, but also for spiritual purposes. The Bible mentions our eyes, lips (mouth and tongue), and cheeks. I believe God intends us to move beyond the physical realm into the spiritual realm to gain His perspective on numerous topics. Please allow me some latitude as I present three of our facial features, how I apply my makeup to each one. Scriptures from the Bible illustrate how we use these features to express God's love and His character, so that He alone will receive the ultimate glory.

I begin my makeup regiment by applying foundation to my skin to create a smooth, evenly colored surface onto which the rest of my makeup will adhere. I'm old school when it comes to makeup, and I still use loose face powder because I prefer a matte finish. I have extremely fair skin, which comes off as pale and pasty-white; therefore, it is essential that I accentuate my features with lots of color. God's Word should be the foundation of our lives. Beginning each day reading the Word of God creates a solid foundation on which to build my life. It is necessary that I commune with My Father in Heaven daily because I gain wisdom, understanding, and strength to go about my day doing His will for my life. Every event and experience in my life will only glean meaning, be enhanced with joy, and fulfill my purpose here on earth if my actions and attitudes are founded on His Word.

> Could there be any other god like you? You are the only God to be worshipped, for there is not a more secure foundation to build my life upon than you. Psalm 18:31 (TPT)

Our Lips

My lips are the first feature that I tackle. I always line my lips with a lip liner, always, for this is one of Sue Ann's non-negotiable rules. Lipliner defines our lips and accentuates the shape of our mouth; it also keeps lipstick in its place, so it doesn't bleed or smear outside our lip area. My beloved Bobbi Brown Burnt Red #9 is my signature look, the deep red color draws attention to my mouth. I have thin lips, so I try to line them and fill them in as much as possible to make them look as full as I can. It's funny to me that I have such thin lips but such a big mouth, and I'm not talking about the measurable size; I'm talking about the fact that I talk a lot, probably too much. But we'll talk about that later.

Our lips frame our mouth, our lips give our mouth shape. Lipliner defines our lips like God's Word defines our speech! Our lipstick provides color to enhance and accentuate our lips as God's Word gives encouragement and life to others. We use our lips to praise God and it is vitally important to guard our words and what we say. The words that come out of our lips (mouth) will also frame our lives.

Let's look at some Scriptures that illustrate the many purposes of our lips, mouth, and tongue (voice).

Speaking:

In Exodus 4:11 we see Moses arguing with God to give the task of speaking to the Israelites to someone else, "The Lord said to him, 'Who gave human beings their mouths? ... Is it not I, the Lord?'" (NIV)

Even Job in his crushing distress purposefully said, "As long as I have life within me, the breath of God in my nostrils, my lips will not say anything wicked, and my tongue will not utter lies." Job 27:3-4 (NIV)

Psalm 17:1 ...I've done what's right and my lips speak truth... (TPT)

Psalm 19:14 May these words of my mouth and this meditation of my heart be pleasing in your sight, Lord, my Rock and my Redeemer. (NIV)

Proverbs 16:1 The preparations of the heart belong to man, but the answer of the tongue is from the Lord. V. 13 Righteous lips are the delight of kings, and they love him who speaks what is right. (NKJV)

Praising:

Psalm 33:1 It's time to sing and shout for joy! Go ahead, all you redeemed ones, do it! Praise him with all you have, for **praise** looks lovely on the lips of God's lovers. (TPT)

Psalm 51:15 O Lord, open my lips, that my mouth may declare Your **praise**. (AMP)

Psalm 63:3 Because your lovingkindness is better than life, My lips shall **praise** You. (NKJV)

Psalm 119:171 Let my lips utter **praise**, for you teach me your statutes. (NKJV)

Psalm 147:1 Hallelujah! **Praise** the Lord! How beautiful it is when we sing our **praises** to the beautiful God; for **praise** makes you lovely before him and brings him great delight! (TPT)

Psalm 34:1 Lord! I'm bursting with joy over what you've done for me! My lips are full of perpetual **praise**. (TPT)

Hebrews 13:15 Through Jesus, therefore, let us continually offer to God a sacrifice of **praise** – the fruit of lips that openly profess his name. (NIV)

Guarding our lips:

Psalm 141:3 God give me grace to **guard my lips** from speaking what is wrong. (TPT)

Proverbs 2:24 Keep your mouth free of perversity; keep corrupt talk far from your lips. (NIV)

Proverbs 5:1-2 My son [and daughter], pay attention to my wisdom, turn your ear to my words of insight, that you may maintain discretion and your lips may preserve knowledge. (NIV)

Proverbs 13:2-3 From the fruit of their lips people enjoy good things, but the unfaithful have an appetite for violence. Those who **guard their lips** preserve their lives, but those who speak rashly will come to ruin. (NIV)

Proverbs 21:23 Watch your words and be careful what you say, and you'll be surprised how few troubles you'll have. V.28 …but the **guarded words** of an honest man stand the test of time. (TPT)

Encouragement:

Proverbs 10:32 Words that bring delight pour from the lips of the godly, … (TPT)

Proverbs 16:24 Gracious words are a honeycomb, sweet to the soul and healing to the bones. (NIV)

Proverbs 31:26 Her teachings are filled with wisdom and kindness as loving instruction pours from her lips. (TPT)

Speaking the truth:

Proverbs 12:14 From the fruit of their **lips** people are filled with good things. V. 19 **Truthful lips** endure forever, but a lying tongue lasts only a moment. (NIV)

Proverbs 14:3b …but the **lips** of the wise protect them. (NIV)

I John 3:18 My little children, let us not love in word or in tongue, but in deed and in **truth**! (NKJV)

Repercussion of your words:

Proverbs 18:21 The tongue has the **power of life and death**, and those who love it will eat its fruit. (NIV)

The AMP version says, "Death and life are in the power of the tongue, And those who love it and indulge it will eat its fruit and **bear the consequences** of their words."

Proverbs 13:2-3 From the fruit of their **lips** people enjoy good things, but the unfaithful have an appetite for violence. Those who **guard**

their lips preserve their lives, but those who speak rashly will come to ruin. (NIV)

Sharing the Gospel:

2 Corinthians 5:20 We are ambassadors of the Anointed One who carry the message of Christ to the world, as though God were tenderly pleading with them directly through our **lips**. So we tenderly plead with you on Christ's behalf, "Turn back to God and be reconciled to him." (TPT)

Pucker up:

Besides speaking, we use our lips to pucker up for a kiss. In The Passion Translation, the book, Song of Solomon begins with the Shulamite woman speaking of Solomon, "Let him kiss me with the kisses of his mouth- For your love is better than wine." We see a beautiful picture of Solomon and his love. "Your face is lovely. Your **lips** are as lovely as Rahab's scarlet ribbon, speaking mercy, speaking grace. The words of your mouth are as refreshing as an oasis. What pleasure you bring to me!" In the NIV version it says, "Your lips are like a strand of scarlet, and your mouth is lovely. Your lips, O my spouse drip as the honeycomb; honey and milk are under your tongue." These lovers speak to each other through psalms and hymns as each one verbalizes their affection and attraction to one another. Solomon admired the woman's character just as much as her beauty.

Our Eyes

Let's move on to my eyes, which in my opinion, are my best feature. My eyes are small and somewhat slanted; they are categorized as *the beautiful oriental eye*, or so says the Facial Structure Manual that Sue Ann referred to during our modeling classes. I tend to line my eyes with black eyeliner and use the blackest black mascara I can find to make my eyes appear larger. I also use gold or copper colored eyeshadow on my eyelids to accentuate the blue in my eyes.

They say that our eyes are the windows into our soul. I'm not sure if I entirely understand what that means, but I do know that our eyes have many functions. The first and most obvious use of our eyes is to see; our sight is vital to experiencing our world. We read with our eyes, we perceive with our eyes, and we take in and admire all of God's creation with our eyes. If you've ever studied the anatomical features and functions of the eye, you would marvel at the sophistication and intricacies of each part, and how all of the parts work together to form what we call *sight*. Eye color variation is also quite interesting; my mom, one of my brothers and I all have blue eyes, but each set is a distinct color blue from the other. The same goes for my dad and my youngest brother who tend to have a bit of green mixed in with the blue in their eyes. God created each one of our eye colors unique, and I'm positive there are billions of colors on the eye color spectrum.

Let us look at what the Bible says about **eyes**:

2 Chronicles 16:9 For the **eyes** of the Lord run to and fro throughout the whole earth, to show Himself strong on behalf of those whose heart is loyal to Him. (NKJV)

I Peter 3:12 For the **eyes** of the Lord are on the righteous and His ears are attentive to their prayer, but the face of the Lord is against those who do evil. (NKJV)

Song of Solomon 1:15 You have dove's **eyes**. 4:1 You have dove's **eyes** behind your veil. V.9 You have ravished my heart with one look of your **eyes**. (NKJV)

Proverbs 7:2 If you do what I say you will live well. Guard your life with my revelation-truth, for my teaching is as precious as your eyesight. (TPT)

Keep my commands and you will live; guard my teachings as the apple of your **eye**. Proverbs 7:2 (NIV)

Proverbs 20:12 The hearing ear and the seeing **eye**, the Lord has made them both. (NKJV)

Psalm 94:9 God isn't blind! He who made the **eye** has superb vision and he's watching all that you do. (TPT)

Psalm 17:8 Protect me from harm, keep an **eye** on me like you would a child reflected in the twinkling of your **eye.** (TPT)

Psalm 25: 6-7 Give me grace, Lord! Always look at me through your **eyes** of love – your forgiving eyes of mercy and compassion. When you think of me, see me as one you love and care for. (TPT)

Proverbs 15:30 **Eyes** that focus on what is beautiful bring joy to the heart, and hearing a good report refreshes and strengthens the inner being. (TPT)

Psalm 119:18 Open my **eyes**, that I may behold wonderful things from Your law. (NIV)

Psalm 121:1 I will lift my **eyes** to the mountains; from where shall my help come? (NIV)

Matthew 13:16 But blessed [spiritually aware, and favored by God] are your **eyes,** because they see; and your ears, because they hear. I assure you and most solemnly say to you, many prophets and righteous men [who were honorable and in right standing] longed to see what you see, and did not see it, and to hear what you hear, and did not hear it. (Jesus' words about the parable of the seed and the sower.) (AMP)

Luke 11:34-35 The **eye** is the lamp of your body. When your **eye** is clear [spiritually perceptive, focused on God], your whole body also is full of light [benefiting from God's precepts]. But when it is bad [spiritually blind], your body also is full of darkness [devoid of God's word]. Be careful, therefore, that the light that is in you is not darkness. (AMP)

Ephesians 1:18-20 And [I pray] that the **eyes of your heart** [the very center and core of your being] may be enlightened [flooded with the light by the Holy Spirit], so that you will know and cherish the hope [the divine guarantee, the confident expectation] to which He has called you, the riches of His glorious inheritance in the saints [God's people], and [so that you will begin to know] what the immeasurable and unlimited and surpassing greatness of His [active, spiritual] power is in us who believe. (AMP)

I pray that God will give us eyes to see the glory of the Lord, and to see others as Jesus sees them. God wants us to keep our eyes fixed on Him as he guides us through our lives. He also wants us to see people as He does, through the eyes of love, empathy, compassion, encouragement, and grace.

> I love this quote by Audrey Hepburn, "For beautiful eyes look for the good in others, for beautiful lips speak only words of kindness, and for poise walk with the knowledge that you are never alone."

Our Cheeks

A smile is the best makeup a girl can wear.
—Marilyn Monroe

As I've mentioned, I have extremely fair skin, so putting on blush is essential to give some color to my face. Lastly, when putting on my makeup, I dust the apple of my cheeks with brightly colored blush, so that when I smile my face lights up and others see the joy I carry inside.

I came across a short article in *People* magazine (May 14, 2018) about the famous performer and writer, Carol Burnett. She spoke about her dearly beloved daughter, Carrie, who was diagnosed with lung cancer in her 30's which then spread to her brain. Before her death in 2002, Carrie spoke of her legacy, "Our legacy is really the lives we touch. More than anything, we are remembered for our **smiles**- the ones we share with our closest and dearest and the ones we bestow on a total stranger who needed it right then, and God put us there to deliver."

Song of Solomon 1:10 Your **cheeks** are lovely with ornaments, your neck with chains of gold. (NKJV)

Song of Solomon 5:13 His **cheeks** are like a bed of balsam, banks of sweet- scented herbs; His lips are lilies dripping with liquid myrrh. (NASB 1995)

Unfortunately, many of the other scriptures in the Bible that mention cheeks are not associated with love and kindness, but with mourning, sadness, and being struck *on the cheek*.

For example, in Lamentations 1:2 it says, "She weeps bitterly in the night, her tears are on her **cheeks**; among all her lovers she has none to comfort her. All her friends have dealt treacherously with her, they have become her enemies" (NKJV).

To him who strikes you on the one cheek, offer the other also. And from him who takes away your cloak, do not withhold your tunic either. Luke 6:29 (NKJV)

The order in which you put your makeup on doesn't really matter, just be sure you apply His Word everyday, so that you are equipped to go out into this world prepared for life, as God transforms you into the godly woman that He wants you to become.

I'd like to give a shout out to the Dove Soap Beauty campaign; their commercials about the diversity of beauty are so inspiring. Multi-cultural and multi-ethnic women with varying body types and skin color are represented, instead of the stereotypical woman we see in other commercials marketing name-brand products. Beauty should be all inclusive, not exclusive by only representing a single group of people as the only ones who possess beauty.

The Proverbs 31 woman is who our society should look to as an example of beauty; the scope of her talents and character exudes many facets of her God-given beauty. Possessing God-given talents and carrying out her daily tasks brings her praise and honor from her husband, her children, and others in her community. This is the kind of beauty that we need to celebrate more often.

All this talk about beauty may cause some slight anxiety if you don't view yourself as beautiful. I don't want you, or your daughters, to buy into the notion that beauty is only an outward physical façade. Inner beauty comes from a humble heart filled with love for others, joy, peace, patience, goodness, kindness, faithfulness, gentleness, and self-control which are the *fruits of the Spirit*. Superficial beauty only lasts so long, but inner beauty will last a lifetime. And don't fret if you're one of those gals who lives your life *au naturel* and makeup isn't your forte, remember beauty is in the "eye of the beholder"; your beholder is Christ Jesus, and you are the apple of His eye.

God's Word says in Ephesians 2:10, "For we are God's masterpiece. He created us anew in Christ Jesus, so we can do the good things he planned for us long ago." Wow! Our loving Father calls us His masterpiece! I included this scripture because I love art! Painters like Van Gogh, Picasso, Mondrian, and others were all struggling and starving artists until someone in the art world attached value to their paintings. As their artwork became known and appreciated the value of their work rose in unimaginable monetary value. Art collectors often pay exorbitant amounts of money for the pleasure of owning what the world labels "a masterpiece." If their art pieces have sold for millions of dollars, and our Maker calls us His masterpiece, then we must be extremely valuable to Him.

Be yourself! Because an original is always worth more than a copy. —Suzy Kassem

Make sure you remind your daughters, "… your renown went forth among the nations because of your beauty, for it was perfect through the splendor that *I had bestowed on you*, declares the Lord God" Ezekiel 16:14 (ESV).

Recall with me the story of Moses in the book of Exodus 34:29-35 when he goes to the top of Mount Sinai for 40 days and 40 nights, eking out the Ten Commandments. "When Moses came down from Mount Sinai with the two tablets of the covenant law in his hands, he was not aware that his face was radiant because he had spoken with the Lord. When Aaron and all the Israelites saw Moses, his face was radiant, and they were afraid to come near him." We learn that during each time Moses spoke with the Israelites, he placed a veil over his face. And each time that he revisited the Lord on the mountain, he removed the veil when in the presence of God. Again, in verse 35 we are told, "they saw his face was radiant" (NIV).

I genuinely believe, no amount of makeup can make a woman's face as beautiful, or as radiant, as a woman who sits in the presence of the Lord.

Those who look to him are radiant, and their faces shall never be ashamed.

Psalm 34:5 (ESV)

Perfection is an elusive standard of beauty, and the standard keeps changing. Beauty is now filtered, photoshopped, and deceptively allures young girls into the trap of comparison. Anna Wintour, editor-in-chief of *Vogue* magazine, is not the ultimate authority on beauty. Rumor has it that she makes or breaks modeling careers with the phrase, "not enough." Not tall enough, not skinny enough, not exotic enough, not pretty enough; you fill in the blank. Sisters in Christ you are enough! The only opinion that matters is God's opinion which is based on His great love for us. "See what great love the Father has lavished upon us, that we should be called children of God! And that is what we are! The reason the world does not know us is that it did not know him" I John 3:1 (NIV). "Your beauty should not come from outward adornment, such as elaborate hair styles and the wearing of gold jewelry or fine clothes. Rather, it should be that of your inner self, the unfading beauty of the gentle and quiet spirit, which is of great worth in God's sight. For this is the way the holy women of the past who put their hope in God used to adorn themselves" 1 Peter 3:2-5 (NIV).

GOD'S WORD IS TRUTH

Heaven and earth will disintegrate before even the smallest detail of the Word will fail or lose its power. Luke 16:17 (TPT)

What is truth? Is it something we decide? Is it something society decides? Is it something God decides? Who defines truth in our lives? As God's creations we need to have a firm and decisive understanding of what truth is and who defines that truth. In John 1:1 it says, "In the beginning was the Word, and the Word was with God, and the Word was God" (NIV). God and His Word are the same. Therefore, as believers we must accept God's Word as truth. The Bible is our guidebook for living in this world. I read somewhere that B-I-B-L-E stands for Basic Instructions Before Leaving Earth. I'm not sure if that's accurate or someone made that up, but it's a very creative acronym. From Genesis to Revelation, the Bible is filled with stories of human beings stumbling around on earth attempting to do what is right and maintain communion with God, and failing miserably. Scriptures reveal God's character of love, grace, mercy, patience, wisdom, and kindness. Some people look at the Bible as just another book, having no more importance than an encyclopedia, a novel, a history textbook, or the phone book. However, "All scripture is God-breathed and is useful for teaching, rebuking, correcting, and training in righteousness, so that the servant of God may be thoroughly equipped for every good work" 2 Timothy 3:16-17 (NIV).

If we do not accept God's Word as the standard by which we live our lives, then what standard will we use to gauge our behavior as right or wrong, or our thoughts as godly or ungodly, or our beliefs as based on truth or falsehoods?

> "…without God as an ultimate standard of truth, without "objective" truth that is the same for everyone, all we have are "truths" as interpreted by individuals." –Brett McCracken

> Psalm 12:6 states, "For every word God speaks is sure and every promise is pure" (TPT).

> God's Word is perfect in every way; how it revives our souls! His laws lead us to truth, and his ways change the simple into wise. His teachings make us joyful and radiate his light; his precepts are so pure! His commands, how they challenge us to keep close to his heart! The revelation-light or his Word makes my spirit shine radiant. Everyone of the Lord's commands are right; following them brings cheer. Nothing he says ever needs to be changed. The rarest treasures of life are found in his truth. That's why I prize God's Word like others prize the finest gold. Nothing brings such sweetness as seeking his living words. Psalm 19:7-12,14 (TPT)

> The sum total of all your words adds up to absolute truth, and every one of your righteous decrees is everlasting. Psalm 119:160 (TPT)

As believers we must choose to accept God's Word as truth, or we will be deceived. As mothers, we must teach our daughters to hear God's voice, read His Word, study His Word, memorize His Word, and to believe with every fiber of their being that God's Word is true, and His Word is the ultimate authority in their lives. My goal is to impart God's Word to my daughters and cover them with prayer as they grow and develop. I want my daughters to know what God's Word says about them and who He created them to be.

Somethings we should know about the Word of God:

For the Word of God is living and powerful, and sharper than any two-edged sword, piercing even to the division of soul and spirit, and of joints and marrow, and is the discerner of the thoughts and intents of the heart. Hebrews 4:12 (NKJV)

As for God, His way is perfect; the word of the Lord is flawless. He is a shield to all who trust in Him. 2 Samuel 22:31 (NIV)

Let's start from the beginning; In Genesis Chapter 2, God created Adam and Eve. They were truly blessed because their relationship was based on face-to-face interactions with the living God. How incredible and incomprehensible! The Garden of Eden was a luscious paradise with flora and fauna beyond our wildest imaginations, but a reality for Adam and Eve. They wanted for nothing, but as human nature would have it, in Chapter 3 they made a bad decision and lost it all.

Let's look at the story:

Now the serpent was more cunning than any beast of the field which the Lord God had made. And he said to the woman, "Has God indeed said, 'You shall not eat of every tree of the garden'?" And the woman said to the serpent, "We may eat the fruit of the trees of the garden, but of the fruit of the tree which is in the midst of the garden, God has said, 'You shall not eat it, nor shall you touch it, lest you die.'" Then the serpent said to the woman, "You will not surely die. For God knows that in the day you eat of it your eyes will be opened and you will be like God, knowing good and evil." So when the woman saw that the tree *was* good for food, that it was pleasing to the eyes, and a tree desirable to make *one* wise, she took of its fruit and ate. She also gave to her husband with her, and he ate. Then the eyes of both of them were opened, and they knew they *were* naked; and they sewed fig leaves together and made themselves coverings. Genesis 3:1-6 (NKJV)

So, as we see Eve was deceived by the serpent (Satan) and her decision to eat the fruit that God said was *off limits* led to the fall of man. Yes, Adam was just as guilty because he also sinned, but we are going to focus on Eve for now. Eve represents our daughters; she was the first daughter of God. If the very first daughter was deceived by Satan then we have to make sure our daughters are aware of his schemes, teaching them to recognize and reject any lie that comes from him. Oh, I can assure you, Satan is going to tempt your beloved daughters and try to deceive them.

In 1 Peter 5:8 we are warned to, "Be alert and of sober mind. Your enemy the devil prowls around like a roaring lion looking for someone to devour." And in John 10:10 we read, "The thief does not come except to steal, and to kill, and to destroy. I [Jesus] have come that they may have life, and that they may have it more abundantly" (NKJV). I am not referencing these Bible scriptures to scare you or your daughters; I don't want fear to grip their hearts and think that they are hunted prey. I firmly believe that as long as our daughters have the Word of God securely planted in their hearts, they will be strengthened, encouraged, and ready when those situations arise that challenge their faith and their beliefs; they will be able to "cast down every argument [imagination] and every high thing that exalts itself against the knowledge of God, bringing every thought into captivity to the obedience of Christ" 2 Corinthians 10:5 (NKJV).

> One well- known and extremely influential English Baptist Preacher, Charles Spurgeon once stated, "Consider how precious a soul must be, when both God and the devil are after it."

Let us look at a few scriptures that tell us what God says about his love for our daughters, how precious and valuable they are to him, and how much he cares for them. Of course, this list is not exhaustive because God's love is infinite, but it will give you a starting place to begin instilling God's Word into your daughters' hearts and minds.

Before I formed you in the womb I knew you, before you were born I set you apart. Jeremiah 1:5 (NIV)

The Lord appeared to us in the past, saying: "I have loved you with an everlasting love; I have drawn you with unfailing kindness." Jeremiah 31:3 (NIV)

Because of the Lord's great love we are not consumed, for his compassions never fail. They are new every morning; great is your faithfulness. Lamentations 3:22 (NIV)

For the Lord's training of your life is the evidence of his faithful love. And when he draws you to himself, it proves you are his delightful child. Hebrews 12:6-7 (TPT)

He kept him as the apple of His eye; Hide me under the shadow of Your wings. Deuteronomy 32:10 (NKJV)

Keep me as the apple of Your eye; Hide me under the shadow of Your wings. Psalm 17:8 (NKJV)

Psalm 86:15 But you, O Lord, are a God merciful and gracious, slow to anger and abounding in steadfast love and faithfulness. (ESV)

For He shall give His angels charge over you, to keep you in all your ways. Psalm 91:11 (NKJV)

Your hands have made me and fashioned me; give me understanding, that I may learn Your commandments. Psalm 119:73 (NKJV)

For you formed my inward parts; You covered me in my mother's womb. I will praise You, for I am fearfully *and* wonderfully made. Marvelous are Your works. And *that* my soul knows very well. My frame was not hidden from You, When I was made in secret, *And* skillfully wrought in the lowest parts of the earth. Your eyes saw my substance, being yet unformed. And in Your book, they all were written, The days fashioned for me, When as yet there were none of them. Psalm 139:13-16. (NKJV)

But now, O Lord, You are our Father; we are the clay, and You our potter; And all we *are* the work of Your hand. Isaiah 64:8 (NKJV)

For thus says the Lord of hosts: "He sent me after glory, to the nations which plunder you; for he who touches you touches the apple of His eye" Zachariah 2:8. (NKJV)

Fear not, for I have redeemed you; I have called you by name, you are mine. Isaiah 43:1 (ESV)

If you, then, though you are evil, know how to give good gifts to your children, how much more will your Father in heaven give good gifts to those who ask him! Matthew 7:11 (NIV)

And even the very hairs of your head are all numbered. Matthew 10:30 (NIV)

Are not five sparrows sold for two copper coins? And not one of them is forgotten before God. But the very hairs of your head are all numbered. Do not fear, therefore; you are of more value than many sparrows. Luke 12:6-7 (NKJV)

Yet to all who did receive him, to those who believed in his name, he gave the right to become children of God – children born not of natural descent, nor of human decision or a husband's will, but born of God. John 1:12-13 (NIV)

The Spirit himself testifies with our spirit that we are God's children. Romans 8:16 (NIV)

For we are God's masterpiece. He has created us anew in Christ Jesus, so we can do the good things he planned for us long ago. Ephesians 2:10 (NLT)

The Lord your God is with you, the Mighty Warrior who saves. He will take great delight in you; in his love he will no longer rebuke you, but will rejoice over you with singing. Zephaniah 3:17 (NIV)

But the Lord is faithful, who will establish you and guard you from the evil one. 2 Thessalonians 3:3 (NKJV)

But we are bound to give thanks to God always for you, brethren beloved by the Lord, because God from the beginning chose you for salvation through sanctification by the Spirit and belief in the truth, … Therefore, brethren, stand fast and hold the traditions which you were taught, whether by word or our epistle. 2 Thessalonians 2:13-15 (NKJV)

But you are a chosen people, a royal priesthood, a holy nation, God's special possession, that you may declare the praises of him who called you out of darkness into his wonderful light. 1 Peter 2:9 (NIV)

The NIV version states, "See what great love the Father has lavished upon us, that we should be called children of God!"; this reminds me of the song "Speechless" by Steven Curtis Chapman.

And finally, His ultimate act of love for us we find in John 3:16 "For God so loved the world that he gave his only begotten son, that whosoever believes in him, should not perish but have everlasting life" (NKJV). Also written in Romans 5:8, "But God demonstrated His own love towards us, in that while we were still sinners, Christ died for us" (NKJV). The Creator of life loves you so intensely that He allowed His son to die in your place before you ever repented. Now that deserves a Hallelujah!

There are innumerable messages being transmitted throughout the earth via social media, television, radio, magazines, movies, peer groups, and even religious groups. Much of this information can be misinformation and confusing depending on the source. I do not want my daughters to be confused about anything, but especially what God says about them.

In The Passion Translation of James 1:22-25 there is excellent advice for our daughters, "Don't just listen to the **Word** of **Truth** and not respond to it, for that is the essence of *self-deception*. So always let his **Word** become like poetry written and fulfilled by your life! If you listen to the **Word** and don't live out the message you hear, you become like a person who looks in the mirror of the **Word** to discover the reflection of his face in the beginning. You *perceive how God sees you* in the mirror of the **Word**, but then you go out and *forget your divine origin*. But those who set their gaze deeply into the perfecting law of liberty are fascinated by and respond to **the truth**. They hear and are strengthened by it – they experience God's blessing in all that they do!" I have italicized and emboldened several words and phrases to magnify the significance of this passage.

Our divine origin is in Almighty God and His Word enables us to see ourselves as He sees us. I know that every mother out there wants her daughter to see herself the way God sees her: loved, a child of the King, beautiful, smart, talented, fun, funny, creative, possessing all the wonderful qualities that God has woven into her personality before she was even born.

One of my all-time favorite songs is "**You Say**" by Lauren Daigle. It is an amazing anthem for all God's children, but especially His daughters. When I am doubting myself or have lost confidence, I play this song on my iPhone and sing along pretending to be one of Lauren's backup singers. There have been days when I've played this song twenty times, or until the message eventually sunk in. "**You Say**" encourages and uplifts my heart; you should check it out. Below are a few lines from Lauren's song that particularly resonate with me.

You Say

by Lauren Daigle

I keep fighting voices in my mind that say I'm not enough/
Every single lie that tells me I will never measure up/
Remind me once again just who I am because I need to know/
The only thing that matters now is everything You think of me/
In You I find my worth, in You I find my identity/
You say I am loved when I can't feel a thing/
When I don't belong, oh You say I am Yours/
And I believe.
Songwriters: Jason Ingram, Lauren Daigle, Paul Brendon Mabury, and Mike Donehey

Another fantastic song to boost your mood and strengthen your resolve that Jesus' voice is the only one you should believe is "**Voice of Truth**" by Casting Crowns.

Voice of Truth

by

Casting Crowns

But the waves are calling out my name and they laugh at me/
Reminding me of all the times I've tried before and failed/
The waves they keep telling me/
Time and time again, "Boy, you'll never win!"/
But the voice of truth tells me a different story/
And the voice of truth says, "Do not be afraid!"/
And the voice of truth says, "This is for My glory"/
I will choose to listen and believe the voice of truth.

I have no greater joy than to hear that my children are walking in truth.
3 John 1:4 (NIV)

UNIQUENESS

Encouraging our daughters to embrace their uniqueness…

Today You Are You!
That is Truer than True!
There is no one alive who is
You-er Than You!
Dr. Seuss

Being in education for twenty years has afforded me the pleasure and opportunity to read many books written by Dr. Seuss; he was definitely ahead of his time regarding children's literature. His books were filled with imaginative characters, unheard of before: the Sneetches, the Lorax, Thing 1 and Thing 2, and Glotzs. I believe he purposefully created these one-of-a-kind characters so his readers could relate to the ideal that we are not all alike, but different in so many ways. I think that Dr. Seuss wanted his readers to embrace and be proud of their individuality. Imagined if we all looked alike, carbon copies of each other; how boring would our world be? Imagine if there was only one color of crayon, or nail polish, fabric, or flower, the world would be so bland and boring.

Our society tends to place people in neat little boxes. If you look like "A" you are accepted and if you look like "B" you are rejected. Rejection doesn't feel good and causes us to have an inaccurate view of ourselves. As we discussed earlier in the book, our view of ourselves should be based on what God, our maker, says about us, not society. As an educator, I must recognize the differences in my students and how they learn. Differential learning is huge in education because not all students learn in the same way. Teachers diversify their lessons to meet each student's need; this is quite a challenge, but I've always tried to do my best for every child. These days teachers also have to meet the psychological, social, and emotional needs of their students.

At the beginning of each school year, I read *You Are Special* by Max Lucado, to my students. I want my students to know that I love them and appreciate their unique personalities and character traits. I've included a short summary of *You Are Special*.

In the beginning of the book, we are introduced to a village of wooden people known as Wemmicks; each Wemmick was carved by Eli, a woodworker, whose workshop sat on a hill overlooking the village. Each Wemmick was different, having distinct features, clothing, and stature. The Wemmicks lived by a value system; they received either gold stars or gray dots, depending on their appearance and abilities. Receiving stars made the Wemmicks feel good about themselves, but receiving dots made them feel bad about themselves.

Next, we are introduced to Punchinello, a Wemmick who is covered in gray dots. Punchinello's self-esteem has been greatly affected by all the dots other Wemmicks have stuck on him. He is not talented in any way, and he has scratches on his wood; he desperately wants to be good enough and accepted by the other wooden people, but he sees himself as tarnished.

Then one day Punchinello meets Lucia, a Wemmick with no stars or dots. He wonders how this is possible. Lucia explains that she goes to see Eli, The Woodcarver, every day. So, at Lucia's urging, Punchinello, although hesitant but curious, goes to see Eli. As Punchinello looks around the workshop, someone calls out his name. As he turns around, he sees Eli, The Woodcarver. "You know my name?" Punchinello asks. "Of course, I do", said Eli, "I made you." "…you are special because I made you. And I don't make mistakes." During their meaningful heart-to-heart, Eli explains, "I don't care what the other Wemmicks think, and you shouldn't either."

Punchinello finally realizes that the only opinion of him that really mattered was Eli's opinion.

I hope you will take time to read the story in its entirety, because this brief summary does not do the book justice. Read it to your children or grandchildren, they will absolutely love it. Or read it for your own pleasure; even a children's book can touch the heart of an adult in the most simple but profound way.

Don't be like the rest of them *darling*.
            –Coco Chanel

I genuinely appreciate the ideal of being different, or as I prefer to be called "unique." My husband didn't know what he was getting himself into when he married me; my dad warned him, but he wasn't dissuaded. Brad thought I was going to be a traditional wife, or at least the stereotypical one that he created in his head; you know, the one who enjoys cooking, cleaning, growing plants, working in the garden, and taking part in DIY projects. Nope, not this chick. I think it took him about fifteen years to come to the realization that I wasn't *that* wife. I was different, very different, and I probably wasn't going to change. Instead of calling me "weird," which I didn't like and took as an insult, he eventually changed his vernacular and started referring to me as "unique," which I appreciated much more.

My daughters, Sarah and Sophie, are identical twins, scientifically known as monozygotic twins, resulting from the fertilization of a single egg that splits in two. My girls shared the same placenta and embryonic sac; fortunately, there was a thin membrane that separated the babies which helped to keep them from becoming entangled in the other ones' umbilical cord. Identical twins sometimes experience "twin to twin transfer" in utero, resulting in one baby taking all the nourishment from the mother, and the other baby ends up not getting the adequate nourishment it needs to grow and develop. Thank the good Lord Sarah and Sophie did not experience this, or have any complications during gestation.

Identical twins share the exact same DNA and when genetically tested, the results are a carbon copy of each other. My girls looked exactly alike when they were born, the only difference was that Sophie weighed three ounces more than Sarah, but it was hardly noticeable. As they grew, we noticed a small birthmark on Sarah's lower right jawline that Sophie did not have, and we noticed that Sophie had a large distinct dimple in her right cheek, which Sarah did not have. So, from the very beginning there were already several physical traits that set them apart from each other.

Many of the differences were so slight, we tagged each baby with ribbons embroidered with each one's name, so that we could tell them apart. We would tag their onesie and then tag their swaddle blanket, and yes, I will admit there were times when I was overcome with distress worrying that I'd tagged the wrong baby with the wrong name. You are probably thinking, how horrible, this lady doesn't even know which child is which? Let me tell you, the stress alone of bringing home two babies from the hospital to take care of at the same time is enough to cause anyone to break out in a sweat.

Not only were there physical differences in Sarah and Sophie, but there were noticeable differences in their personalities. Sarah was calmer as a baby, unlike Sophie who cried a lot. No matter what I would do to soothe her, she still cried, so I would hand her off to Brad. He is much more laid back than I am, and the constant crying didn't seem to bother him as much.

When it came time for the girls to hold their own bottles, another difference became apparent. Sophie would do her best and try to hold her bottle, but Sarah wasn't interested in holding her own bottle and preferred that I hold it for her. I really needed them to learn to hold their own bottles because I had other chores to tend to. So, when Sarah refused to hold her bottle, I would prop it up by putting a small stuffed animal underneath it. She didn't seem to mind this setup, as long as she wasn't the one having to put forth any effort, she was content. Wanting someone else to do it for her became a continuous pattern, and to my regret, still is. I began to see that Sophie was more independent than Sarah and she didn't mind doing things for herself.

Preferences in food, clothing, hair styles, and activities became more evident as the girls have gotten older. Sarah likes red apples and Sophie likes green apples. Sarah likes Coke, Dr. Pepper, or Pepsi and Sophie likes root beer.

Sarah's favorite color was pink, then yellow, and now purple. Sophie's favorite color is blue, and that has never changed. Sarah loves to wear her hair really long, even if it gets in her face, but will also let me put it in a ponytail or braid. Sophie prefers her hair shoulder length, and refuses ponytails or braids, except when I insist she puts it up for her soccer games.

Sarah is my princess who loves dresses, skirts, shirts with ruffled sleeves, sandals, and hoochie-mama shoes. She wears headbands and scrunchies in her hair and will sport a handbag every now and then; her ears are pierced and she loves jewelry. She also takes gymnastics and is working on her back handspring.

Sophie is my "tom girl," she doesn't like to be called a "tom boy" because she *is not a boy*, so we've settled on "tom girl." She prefers athleisure wear, blue jeans, t-shirts, and sneakers. So far, Sophie has not wanted to have her ears pierced, but I'm keeping my fingers crossed. She does wear jewelry, and scrunchies around her wrists, but only agrees to wear a dress for special occasions, for instance, my niece's wedding or school pictures.

Sarah and Sophie also have quite different interests. Sarah is artistic and loves to draw and create, she really has a natural talent which I see in how she styles her clothing. Early on, she wanted to be a fashion designer, but now she is interested in animals and says she wants to be a veterinarian; you should see the band aids and bandages on her stuffed animals.

Sophie has always wanted to be a police officer; she was a police officer for Halloween when she was four years old. That same year for Christmas, my in-laws got the girls electric Jeeps, so Mom and Dad decked out Sophie's with flashing lights, an obnoxiously annoying siren, a deafening bullhorn, and official police badge stickers on the doors of her Jeep. All the kids in our neighborhood have electric cars, so they race around running from Sophie because she tries to give everyone a ticket. Sophie has recently fallen in love with German Shepherds, and she now wants to be the K-9 handler. All I have to say is, whatever vocation my girls decide to pursue, I'll be right there cheering them on.

Two Christmases ago, my girls came home from church with an "Arts and Crafts" project; it was a snowflake made from a large white coffee filter and sparkling glitter. Stapled to the snowflake was a tag with the words, "God Made Me Unique" and the scripture from Psalms 139:14 (NIV) "I praise you because I am fearfully and wonderfully made; your works are wonderful, I know that full well" below the tag. If you have ever read anything about snowflakes, scientifically each snowflake that falls from the heavens is unique, because each one of them follows a slightly different path from the sky to the ground- and thus encountering slightly different atmospheric conditions along the way. The intricate shape of a single arm of the snowflake is determined by the atmospheric conditions experienced by entire ice crystals as they fall. All snowflakes have six arms, each arm an exact replica of the other five arms. Each snowflake is unique, resembling prisms, needles, or lacy patterns. (noaa.gov)

CONFORMITY

Why fit in when you were born to stand out?
—Dr. Seuss

Being an identical twin must be a unique experience in and of itself, as is being the mother of identical twin girls. The world seems fascinated by twins, and my girls continue to garner a lot of attention as they grow older. As they approach double digits in age and they move on to middle school in a few years, I anticipate that they will have to deal with peer pressure. Oftentimes, peer pressure coupled with the need to belong or "fit in," places our still maturing daughters in a position where they will have to make hard choices.

Belonging, as defined by Cambridge Dictionary, is a feeling of being happy or comfortable as part of a particular group and having a good relationship with the other members of the group because they welcome you and accept you. A sense of belonging is one of humanity's most basic emotional needs. As a parent, I immensely want my girls to fit in, to be a part of a group (friends, church, school organizations) in which they are accepted and feel comfortable to be themselves, and who God created them to be (not an altered version of themselves). Such groups should be supportive of their goals, interests, and activities, and challenge them to "be the light" in every situation.

Unfortunately, if our children are not grounded in the Gospel and confident of their identity in Christ, they may falter, and become persuaded to engage in behaviors and activities that are contradictory to their belief system; ones that will draw them away from God and lead to unfortunate consequences. God's Word gives our children confidence to stand up for what is right instead of being tempted to "follow the crowd" and do what everyone else is doing. I want Sarah and Sophie to have the courage to stand up for what is right, even if they are standing alone. I want them to maintain their unique individual personalities and still enjoy being a part of something bigger than themselves.

Another terrific book by Max Lucado, *If Only I Had a Green*

Nose, deals with the ever changing world of fads and belonging, and how they entice people [our children] to conform just to fit in, but ultimately causing them self-doubt. The summary states, "Why would he (Punchinello) want that (a green nose) when he knows Eli made each of them different for a reason? Punchinello needed to hear his Maker say, 'I'll always help you be who I made you to be.'"

Interesting research on Conformity in Teenagers

Conformity describes shaping actions and beliefs to align with the opinions and behaviors of others. Teens feel pressure to conform during the middle school years because they haven't yet developed a sense of autonomy and tend to struggle with self-esteem and confidence into their high school years.

Abraham Maslow, a noted psychologist, suggested a hierarchy of human needs; one need is the urge to belong and be accepted by family, friends, and peers. Sadly, teens join gangs and cliques and select their friends in an effort to feel a sense of belonging. One obvious way to achieve this feeling of acceptance is by the way they dress and act.

Research indicates that well-adjusted teens develop the ability to make choices about what to think, how to act, and also to make individual decisions, without feeling stress, when these decisions do not conform to peer or society norms, according to the University of Nebraska Lincoln Extension. As mothers, we need to discuss with our daughters alternative choices to conformity.

A Teacher's April Fool's Joke

My friend, Christy Elliott, is a 4th grade English language arts teacher at the same school that Sarah and Sophie attend, and where I helped as the STAAR ELAR interventionist on campus. I worked with several of Mrs. Elliott's students; therefore, I spent a considerable amount of time in her classroom.

Mrs. Elliott thought it would be fun to play an April Fool's joke on her students. I was instantly intrigued after she gave the instructions to the students because the "joke" reminded me of several psychology experiments I've read about on the subject of conformity. She gave them a "test" to see if the students would actually read the directions *completely*, and then follow the directions *accurately;* two skills desperately lacking in our children today.

The test consisted of fifteen questions and the directions were printed at the top of the page. The directions stated, "Read all of the questions before you begin the test." If the students read all the questions carefully, they would only have to print their name at the top of the page and turn in the test. Question 15 was the key to following the directions: it stated, "Write your name at the top of the page. Do not answer questions 1–14. Turn your paper in. Sit back and enjoy the show."

I hate to report, but the students failed the "test" miserably. Instead of reading all 15 questions first, as the directions stated, many immediately began answering each question: #1, #2, #3, and so on. One of the questions directed the students to stand up and do three jumping jacks which some students did, although the teacher had instructed the student not to get out of their seats. Another question directed the students to stand up and shout out the name of their favorite animal, which some students did. And another question directed the students to turn to their neighbor and say, "Howdy, neighbor!," which some did, even though the teacher had also directed them not to talk during the test.

All but three students in the classroom failed the test. I laughed as I watched them act out the instructions on the test, knowing they hadn't read all the questions. As some students acted out the directions, other students who initially appeared to be on the right track began noticing other students doing jumping jacks, or saying "Howdy" to their neighbor, stopped what they were doing, went back to question #1 and began answering the questions.

It was as though those students who were on the right track began to doubt themselves and what they were doing, because other students were doing something different than what the directions stated. Instead of continuing to follow the initial directions, "Read all the questions before you begin the test," these students (who were on the right track) allowed the actions of the other students (who were on the wrong track, and not following directions) to influence their behavior regardless of the explicit instructions from Mrs. Elliott, "Do not get out of your seat and do not talk during the test." Their trajectory changed from being on the right track to getting on the wrong track. Yikes! How easily our children are influenced by their friends and peers. Conformity eclipsed individual thinking, and self-doubt began to permeate the room as the students looked around to see what each other was doing, and then mimicked that behavior.

Going back to our previous discussion about how our daughters see themselves, and their journey to establish a never changing absolute truth regarding their self-worth; we have all been there. As teens, we've been in those situations where peer pressure altered our decisions in-turn affecting our behavior. Yes, we all wanted to fit in. We yearned to belong and be accepted by our friends and peers. Our human nature longs for connection with others, and as teenagers we tend to gravitate toward people that look and think like we do, or who have common interests. I pray that God surrounds my daughters with people who "see them for who they really are," and I hope they are never pressured, manipulated, or coerced to change into someone they're not, just to fit in. Vetting my daughters' friends is a duty I take seriously. While they are still young I have some control over this matter, but as they get older and become teenagers, I'm sure there will be some contentious conversations between my girls and I, if I don't approve of their choice in friends.

AN AUTHOR'S CONFESSION

Charm is deceptive, and beauty is fleeting; but a woman
who fears the Lord is to be praised. Proverbs 31:30 (NIV)

As I sit writing this chapter, my 50th birthday is lurking just around
the corner. The big 5-0!!! Say it isn't so! I've never had a problem
with my age and getting older never really bothered me, but when
I decided to go back to work teaching full-time in August of 2019,
everything in my world turned upside down. Going back into the
classroom at the age of 48 was totally unheard of. I hadn't worked full-
time or had my own classroom in ten years. I knew it would be tough
starting all over again, but for some reason, even though I was hesitant
and maybe a little scared, I felt the need to help.

One day while sitting at gymnastics watching Sarah, I sat talking
with some of the other mothers. Several of them knew that I was a
teacher, and one had heard about a local elementary school in desperate
need of a fourth-grade English teacher. I really wasn't interested in
working full-time because I didn't want to miss out on spending time
with my girls. I had been their homeroom mom when they were in

kindergarten, and I loved being involved at their school. I subbed often that year, and I was able to spend more time with them. The best part was going to school with them every morning and coming home with them every afternoon. Many times, during one of my breaks, I would walk by and peek into their classroom just to get a glimpse of them doing their work or interacting with the other children. I had to wait almost ten years to have these babies, and I didn't want to miss anything in their lives.

I knew taking a full-time job would take some of my time, but I never imagined it would consume my entire life for nine whole months. Setting up a fully functioning classroom three days before school starts is almost impossible, but the Lord gave me supernatural energy and motivation to do this job. I honestly believed this job was an assignment from up above, similar to one He had for me about fifteen years ago, the only difference was *I chose* to take this job, it wasn't forced upon me. Sorry, if I sound somewhat bitter, I'm still working on that.

Little did I know, several unforeseen events would disrupt our school year, make national headlines, and foreshadow "the coming of the end times" with a global pandemic.

In September, hurricane Imelda hit southeast Texas and southwest Louisiana causing damage to structures and flooding like we saw when hurricane Ike hit us one year earlier. In October, our district's on-line automated systems were hacked, and a ransom was paid to return the data. In November, an explosion at the TPC refinery in Port Neches the night before Thanksgiving, blew doors completely off their hinges taking the frames with them, shattered windows, collapsed ceilings, emitted a dangerous gas into the air, and threw hundreds of residents within a four-mile radius into a panic in the middle of the night. My classroom at the time was a portable building which sat on the backside of our school property, less than two blocks away from the refinery. And lastly, the coronavirus.

Covid-19, another name for the coronavirus, was spreading across the globe and people were scared. No one knew anything about Covid-19, or the ramifications of its existence. Our schools shut down and we had to adapt to "our new normal"; learning to set up a Google classroom on-line, integrate that system with our new curriculum, and homeschool our own children. Not to mention, being quarantined in our own homes, businesses closing their doors, and everyday necessities like toilet paper and eggs were in high demand and being auctioned off to the highest bidder. Because of everything we experienced here in southeast Texas, that school year and into the later part of 2020, everyone was anxious, stressed, and overwhelmed. I'm sure if you were to measure the amount of stress experienced by individuals during that time, the score would be off the charts. I sort of went on a tangent there for a minute, but I just wanted all you mothers to know that I completely understand the spectrum of emotions you felt, and I empathize and sympathize with you because I lived it too.

My soul longed for normalcy, and my spirit yearned for something, anything to lift the overshadowing depression that lingered through the summer. My approaching birthday, a major milestone, loomed in the near distance and seemed to mock me, "Half a century old." These words echoed through my mind reminding me that I was no longer young. My amazing friend, Angie, who is the "friend who sticks closer than a brother [sister]," blessed me with a whimsical hand-painted wine glass prominently displaying the number "50" on the front and a witty saying, "50 is fabulous, and age is just a number" under the very large "50." The glass was covered with an array of brightly colored polka dots and rhinestones. I absolutely loved my gift! It was thoughtful and fun, useful and special and it is proudly displayed in my curio cabinet along with many other treasured pieces of crystal and nick-nacks I've collected through the years.

If you think about it, 50 really *is* just a number. I don't feel 50 years old; my friends and family all tell me I don't look 50 years old. Nevertheless, unwanted changes have come and gone, and I've had no say in the matter. I'm not opposed to change, but growing old gracefully really isn't my thing. Middle age has snuck up on me, and I'm not sure if I like it. I realized I had become uncomfortable in my own skin.

One thing you probably would be surprised to learn is that I am struggling with my own identity, my worth, and my purpose at this time in my life. My flawless porcelain skin has been replaced with fine lines and wrinkles, adult acne, and melasma from massive doses of hormones my body was subjected to as I struggled through six rounds of IVF.

I don't have the ever unpopular "11" a.k.a. angry lines between my eyebrows, it's more like a single slanted line, but still unattractive and unwanted. Multiply lines splay out of the corners of my mouth revealing my true age. My shocking red lipstick that once stayed within the acceptable boundaries of my lip line, now slowly creeps into those lines at the corners of my mouth causing much distress.

Since we are blaming hormones, let's just add to their list of insults; the once willowy 5'8" frame is still 5'8", but now more like a Redwood tree, thicker and sturdier. Of course, I'm talking about the added poundage no woman of any age invites. Twenty pounds you say, that's not so bad. Many would not be alarmed by this amount, but when you compare twenty pounds to the reality that I only gained forty pounds when I was pregnant with my twins, the weight is an unwelcome addition to say the least.

Here I am, authoring a book about the desires and dreams I have for my daughters, desperately wanting them to know their worth in Christ Jesus and base their self-confidence on the Word of God and what He says about them, and *I'm* the one struggling with the concept. And yes, I know the changes that bother me are superficial and will continue to change over time. But thank the good Lord above He speaks to me through His Word, opening my eyes to see the truth about this particular stronghold. I've based much of my self-worth on my physical appearance, rather than on God's word.

The word *stronghold* is defined as a place where a particular cause or belief is strongly defended or upheld. The word *vanity* comes to mind. I remember reading Dr. Nicholas Perricone's book, *The Perricone Prescription*, in which he writes and I'm paraphrasing, "A little bit of vanity is good. People who are vain, tend to take better care of themselves." His sentiment aligned with my thinking, so I assumed the importance

I had placed on my physical appearance wasn't harmful or sinful, and definitely did not constitute a stronghold. However, believing that my appearance is what gave me value or made me worthy of other people's love and acceptance, is all together *a lie*. I'm thankful for His Word as I comb through the pages of the Bible searching for scripture to affirm or deny the thoughts or beliefs I have about myself. His Word sheds light on the truth of his love for me and dispels the lies that whisper, "You are not good enough, you don't measure up, you're not strong enough, you won't win this battle, all your efforts are for naught." When it's hard to comprehend "the overwhelming, never ending, reckless love of God," (words to the song "Reckless Love of God" by Cory Asbury) all we have is our faith to take God at His Word.

I'm going to borrow an illustration from an American Express Credit Card commercial that I believe expresses my love for my daughters, and parallels God loves for you and me perfectly.

Ten years struggling to achieve motherhood.

Six rounds of IVF: $60,000

One month in the NICU: $400,000

Holding Sarah Ashton and Sophie Annabelle, my miracle babies, in my arms for the first time, loving them and kissing their angelic little faces, and calling them *mine*: **Priceless**

This is exactly how God feels about you and me. Our heavenly Father lavishes us with His love because we are priceless to him. Stop, breathe that in, and ponder this awe-inspiring revelation for a few minutes. Soak in his effervescence and let it saturate your soul, new revelation will come, bonds will be broken, and the captive will be set free. Amen and hallelujah!

I mentioned earlier that I'm also struggling with my purpose, my true calling in life. Years ago, when I took a vocational inventory test that matched personality traits and inherent giftings with appropriate professions --teaching was my undeniable calling. Many of my friends were going into education, but I had absolutely no interest in becoming a teacher.

During my freshman year at Texas A&M University, I worked for the Dean of Education, and became acquainted with several of the professors, including a reading professor named Dr. Blaire. During my sophomore year, I decided to take a reading class just to see if my interests had changed, coincidentally Dr. Blaire was teaching the class. All I remember about that course is the professor talked mostly about Basal Readers. I'm embarrassed to tell you, but I skipped that class many times and felt extreme guilt because I knew the professor personally, but maturity was not on my side at that time, and I floundered through my courses until I was forced to choose a major.

While sitting in an Introduction to Psychology class, the guy next to me was looking over his psychology degree plan. As I peered over his shoulder, I realized I had taken the majority of required classes, so right then and there I chose psychology as my major. Thank goodness my genuine curiosity about human behavior kept me interested in the rest of the necessary courses I needed to graduate. I'm proud to say that in May of 1993, I walked across the stage in G. Rollie White Coliseum and received my Bachelor of Science degree in psychology from Texas A&M University.

Now, what was I going to do? I wasn't interested in going to graduate school; I'd finished college in four years, and I was tired. I needed a break, I just wasn't counting on a five-month-long break; no job, no money, talk about being unprepared. I moved back in with my parents until I started my job with The Texas Department of Protective and Regulatory Services, Child Protective Services in October 1993.

I spent five years working for CPS. I honestly loved many aspects of the job; however, there were two specific incidents that left me with Post Traumatic Stress Disorder. That's when I decided that I needed to seek out another job, one that would allow me the opportunity to work with children because I really liked kids. The only option I could think of was teaching. I shrugged my shoulders, applied to be a substitute teacher, and thus began my twenty-year off-and-on-again journey as an educator. You see, when the Lord knows your giftings and allows you to run away from His calling on your life, He always finds a way to put you back on the path that He has chosen for you.

I truly loved teaching for many years. I've switched districts a few times, taught many different grades, and subjects and I have multiple certifications. My dilemma is that all my certifications expired at the end of 2020, and I didn't have enough Continuing Professional Education hours to renew them. No certification equals no job; no job equals no money. So here I sit, wondering what in the world am I supposed to be doing with my life? Should I attend the necessary workshops to have my certifications renewed and go back to teaching full time, or should I take a different path? What if I choose the path to becoming a legitimate author whose books could one day become commercially successful; how strong would my faith have to be? Is this part of God's plan for me? Is writing my new calling?

I have thought about and prayed about *Warpaint* for the past three years. The Lord kept nudging me to get started and to get it written. So once again, I've opened the doors of my heart and shared with you my testimony, along with the hopes and dreams that I have for my daughters. I hope that every mother and every daughter will be blessed beyond measure by the truth I have penned in this book.

In my first book, *WAIT,* I wrote about my struggles with infertility, and how my emotions were so raw during those years, I didn't want to hear about or talk about anything that had to do with the topic of pregnancy. My insecurities caused me to withdraw from family and friends because I knew they didn't understand my situation and they definitely did not understand my pain. I couldn't even be vulnerable with my closest friends. I shut everyone out and suffered silently for a long time. Eventually, God blessed me with Sarah and Sophie, and everything changed; it took a few years to emotionally heal from all the negative emotions I had battled within my mind.

When the time came to write *WAIT*, I contemplated whether to include those chapters about my fertility struggles in the book. I finally felt secure enough to share my testimony, but I winced at the thought of others knowing the explicit, most private details of that painful part of my life, and the specific medical and scientific methodologies I used to achieve motherhood. I knew I would be judged for my choices, and I didn't want that!

Many years ago, I traveled to Houston with a group of women from my church to hear Beth Moore speak. I've read many of her books and completed many of her bible studies, so I'm familiar with her love of delving into the Bible, researching, dissecting, and defining original text materials. She gleans every tiny nugget of truth she can, and she teaches it to us. How blessed we are. Beth radiates God's presence; it's obvious that she spends hours sitting in the presence of our Lord, cultivating their intimate father–daughter relationship.

What I remember most about her talk that night was the demonstration she used with a clear glass vase that was filled with rocks. She emphasized her point by pouring water into the vase; the water filled every empty crevice and space. She explained how our relationship with Jesus needs to be the same. We desperately need Jesus to fill every empty space in our hearts with His love, His Word, and His being. He will occupy and work in every area of your heart if you let him.

Something else Beth mentioned was our requirement as believers to be transparent [the clear glass vase] with others when sharing our testimonies. My interpretation was, "transparency is transforming." The only way to effectively minister to others is if we are *real* with them. If we are fake in our interactions with others, they sense it. Our pretentious façade becomes a wall between the two of us, and the true love of Jesus and the Gospel won't be received, which leaves non-believers the same as they were before they met us. But if we are transparent with others while ministering to them, as we share our testimonies including our failures, our triumphs, and our struggles, they will see our hearts, Jesus' heart. This is when God's love and His Word will go forth and become "life to those who hear it," and their lives will be radically transformed forever.

Just recently, I watched a Netflix documentary about Brene Brown. I'd heard her name mentioned on TV and read a few posts about her on social media, and had heard she was an author, but I didn't realize she was a fellow Texan too. She's an extremely accomplished woman; she earned a Ph.D., is a LMSW, and she continues to research complex abstract emotional human constructs such as vulnerability and what it means to be brave.

She said, "It takes vulnerability to be brave, and it takes braveness to be vulnerable" (and I'm paraphrasing). I hadn't really thought sharing my testimony with the world in *WAIT* meant I was *brave*. I had, however, considered the *vulnerability* aspect of it all; the unknown ramifications of exposing my deepest longings for a child, compounded by the continual heartbreak of my experience. Brene stated that being brave and being vulnerable are on the same end of the spectrum of human behavior and experience, not opposite from one another, which most people inaccurately deduct.

She also said, and I'm paraphrasing again, "anyone who criticized her, for any reason, didn't have the right to, especially if they were not in the arena fighting the battle too." My interpretation and my words, "Those people who sit so comfortably on the sidelines of life as spectators, never having the courage to muck around in the trenches, who piously verbalize their objections and unsolicited opinions, it is those opinions, that in no way matter." I totally agree with her.

I wholeheartedly believe the Lord placed the idea of writing *WAIT*, in my heart many years ago. I only needed to continue living my life and learning some very critical lessons, before I had enough content to compile a book. I can promise you I didn't wake up one morning and say to myself, "Oh, by the way, I think I'll write a book this year." I felt a holy prodding, an assignment from up above, to share my testimony and glorify God in the process. He alone received all the glory; I was only the vessel he had chosen.

I secretly had an ulterior motive for writing *WAIT*; I needed the money, we needed the money. We were thousands of dollars in debt, a result of six rounds of IVF, Sarah and Sophie's one-month-stay in the NICU, the high cost of raising twins, and the fact I was a stay-at-home mom with a meager substitute teaching salary. Although my husband had and still has a great job with a wonderful family-owned company, we were in over our heads. The day our girls were born, we outgrew our house. God knew my *secret motive,* and He knew the intent of my actions seemed justified, in my own mind. "How else could we generate extra income?"

The reality check came when the royalty checks *did not.* God knows me so well, better than I know myself. I was frustrated and didn't understand why my book wasn't flying off the shelves, and why my checking account wasn't going, "Ching, Ching, Ching!" My publishing company was legitimate, but their platform was limited. I had a few book signings at Starbucks and Barnes & Noble, but I came to the sad realization, my book was not going to be a commercial success. So, with a heavy heart, I reached for a cup of coffee and continued on.

One day as I stood in the kitchen, washing dishes and looking out the window, I talked with God, more accurately argued with Him, about the predicament I saw myself in. I said, "God, you know we need a bigger house; Sarah and Sophie are having to share a room. Really? This is 2016, not 1916. They don't have a playroom, and our house is filled with so much kid stuff, we looked like an unorganized storage unit." When I finally stopped griping, the Holy Spirit spoke so gently to my heart, "If I had allowed your book to earn the income you needed, to acquire the house you wanted, you would be completely satisfied and spent the rest of your life being little Suzy Homemaker, and you wouldn't have any motivation to write the next book that I want you to write. *WAIT* was just the *trial run*, to see if you could do it (complete the writing of the book and have it published). Your next book, *Warpaint*, is *the one* I want the world to read." God knows me so well, and again, better than I know myself. With a sigh of resignation, I said, "Okay, okay, so my dream house will have to *wait*." Ironic, don't you think?

So, as I sit here pouring out my heart to you, faithful reader, putting on my bravest face and being vulnerable, my hope is you too will do the same. Know that God will be with you every step of the way on your journey in this chaotic adventure we call *life*. Don't be afraid to tell your story, share your testimony, or be transparent. Our testimony is how we minister to others, and God will be glorified in the process.

DRAMA VS. PEACE

And the peace of God, which transcends all understanding will guard your hearts and your minds in Christ Jesus. Finally, brothers and sisters, whatever is true, whatever is noble, whatever is right, whatever is pure, whatever is lovely, whatever is admirable – if anything is excellent and praiseworthy -think about such things! Philippians 4:6-8 (NIV)

In our household we have five females and one male. My husband is completely outnumbered. With a wife going through menopause, two boisterous nine-year-old daughters, an aged fifteen-year-old Australian Shepherd, a one-year-old Great White Pyrenees, and a five-month-old Siberian Forrest kitten, there's a lot going on. Actually, there is a lot of drama. My girls can go from happy, calm, and compliant to hysterically crying and defiant in six seconds flat! No, I did not time it, I guessed. Most of the time, I'm not even aware what prompted the Jekyll and Hyde transformation, but one thing I know is that this drama becomes exhausting. The peace that permeated the atmosphere has blown out the window and been replaced with anxiety and fear, oftentimes over seemingly benign incidents, without rhyme or reason.

I do not like drama! I grew up in a typically normal, peaceful household. There was no yelling or fighting, or trauma, or drama. I am the first born, so my mom did everything to keep the house quiet when I was a baby, so I would not be awakened from my daily naps. No vacuuming, no blaring TV, no clanging pots, just silence – peaceful silence. Establishing this peaceful atmosphere set a precedent for me for the rest of my life. Now, the only way I can fall asleep at night is with total darkness and total silence. I'll admit, the humming of a steadily running fan is now part of the routine, but for the most part – quietness and peacefulness.

Raising my daughters for the past nine years, I've tried to recreate the same peaceful quiet in my home, but there's just one problem, me! I'm a loud person; when my emotions start to run amuck, I tend to get loud. I must regretfully admit that I've allowed my emotions like anger, exasperation, frustration, exhaustion, anxiety, and fear get the best of me. I tend to holler when I think no one is listening to me. When my girls get upset about something, I tend to meet them at their level of emotion, instead of remaining calm and clear minded. I often end up allowing my emotions to escalate to a level where all peace is gone, and chaos has ensued.

A funny, but not so funny example, is Sarah and Sophie's anxiety over Band-Aids. Yes, they are terrified of Band-Aids! I don't understand their irrational fear, but it started when they were about three years old. When they would fall or scrape their knees, or accidentally injure themselves I'd always offer a Band-Aid to cover their "bobo."

From the beginning they didn't want me to even look at their "bobo," much less doctor it in any way: no hydrogen peroxide, no Neosporin, and especially no Band-Aids. I truly didn't understand this unfounded fear until Sophie, at the age of four, fell and busted her chin wide open on our tile floors. She was riding on a toy backwards and toppled right over; she sat up screaming and holding her chin. Once she let me look, I could see the skin was split and she needed stitches. I called Brad and we met at the Urgent Care clinic.

Sure enough, she needed stitches, but the attending ER physician decided to use Dermabond (medical-grade Super Glue) to glue her chin back together. Then the nurses put an extremely large Band-Aid over the wound to keep the germs out. When we removed the Band-Aid, it traumatized her. I know removing the Band-Aid hurt a little, but you would have thought I was ripping her face off. And poor Sarah, she was a captive audience having a front-row-seat to each event; I know she sensed Sophie's anxiety and internalized it as her own. Being identical twins might explain this, who knows? I blame the overwhelming fear of Band-Aids for causing many drama-filled situations.

Similarly, we had a situation with Sarah that caused a lot of drama. She had a scab on her knee that was hanging by a thread. Normally, I wouldn't suggest she rip it off because the part still attached would hurt when removed, and begin to bleed which would cause a dramatic reaction, a reaction I didn't want to deal with because we were getting dressed to go to Vacation Bible school.

This scab had been hanging all day and I suggested she put a band-aid over it. My reasoning, (which I thought she would understand) was the scab might catch on something and rip off, causing her pain. Secondly, it was quite a large scab and honestly, it was ugly. I told her that no one at VBS would really want to see her scab, thinking I could persuade her to do something about it. She refused the Band-Aid and decided to wear leggings to cover up the scab; however, as she pulled on her leggings, they pulled on the scab, and she began to get upset.

So once again, I suggested a Band-Aid (What was I thinking?) and once again she said, "No!" I'd had enough and I yelled, "Then just get it over with and rip it off!" which horrified her even more. This situation was escalating to a level I did not want to deal with. She didn't like my two options and I couldn't think of another one; after about ten minutes, she conceded and agreed to a Band-Aid. Whoosh!

Finally, the drama would end, but to my dismay, as I walked back into her bedroom with a Band-Aid in hand, Sophie blurted out, "That's the Band-Aid Mom put on my chin, and it hurt *a lot* when she took it off!" I thought, "Thanks a lot Sophie for stirring the pot!" Sarah wailed even louder and refused the Band-Aid once more. It took a few more minutes of convincing, but finally the Band-Aid was on, the leggings were on, both girls were dressed, and we headed out the door to VBS. Just a fun fact: during the summers of 2021 and 2022, my girls attended six Vacation Bible schools, so don't feel guilty Moms if your kids make the rounds to every VBS in town. Our children need *all* the Jesus they can get!

I prayed these situations would arise less often, but my friends with older children say, "It only gets worse." All I can hope for is that I take these powerful scriptures to heart, so when they do arise, *I am the one with more peace in my own heart,* to deal with the circumstances better.

My husband and I would pray for Sarah and Sophie's "bobos" during our nightly prayers, and it finally dawned on me that *fear (and the uncertainty or anticipation of pain)*, not the desire to be dramatic, was the root of these episodes. I began praying the following scriptures over the girls each night. These scriptures covered many situations where *fear* was the issue: thunder and lightning, fear of the dark, fear of sleeping in their bedroom, fear of many things they didn't understand just yet.

> Fear not, for I am with you; be not dismayed, for I am your God; I will strengthen you, I will help you, I will uphold you with my righteous right hand. Isaiah 41:10 (ESV)

> When I am afraid, I put my trust in you. Psalm 56:3 (NIV)

> For God has not given us a spirit of fear, but of power and of love and of a sound mind. 2 Timothy 1:7 (NKJV)

Have I not commanded you? Be strong and courageous. Do not be afraid; do not be discouraged, for the Lord your God will be with you wherever you go. Joshua 1:9 (NIV)

The Lord is with me; I will not be afraid. What can mere mortals do to me? The Lord is with me; he is my helper. Psalm 118:6-7a (NIV)

As Sarah and Sophie get older and mature, we are able to reason with them more. We still struggle with drama now and then, but through wisdom and understanding, we can address the underlying issues and use scripture to cover those situations in prayer, ultimately bringing peace.

I've included some nightly prayers my girls learned when they were tiny tots. I have used condensed versions of the following prayers.

Prayer #1:

God My Friend

God, my friend, it is time for bed
Time to rest my sleepy head.
I pray to you before I do,
Please guide me down the path that's true.

God, my friend, it is time to go,
But before I do I hope you know.
I am thankful for my blessings, too
And God, my friend, I love you!
–Michael J. Edger III

Prayer #2:

For rest and food and loving care,
And all that makes the day so fair.
Help us to do the things we should,
To be to others kind and good,
In all we do, in work or play,
To grow more loving every day.
—Rebecca J. Weston 1885

Prayer #3:

Now I lay me down to rest
I thank the Lord; my life is blessed…
I have my family and my home
And freedom, should I choose to roam.
My days are filled with skies of blue
My nights are filled with sweet dreams too.
I've no reason to beg or plead
I have been given all I need.
—Jill Eisnaugle

Recently, I learned I shouldn't use big words or specific adjectives during prayer time. For one thing, my girls chime in during the prayer to ask about the meanings of certain words, which aggravates me and interrupts my train of thought. Secondly, my children often take words literally instead of figuratively, which also causes much confusion.

One night about halfway through our prayer, I quoted a combination of the two scriptures; John 10:10, "The thief comes only to steal and kill and destroy; I have come that they may have life, and have it to the full," and 1 Peter 5:8, "Be alert and of sober mind. Your enemy the devil prowls around like a roaring lion looking for someone to devour." I was praying for their protection because I want them to feel safe, and

I always incorporate scriptures into my prayers to reassure Sarah and Sophie of the power of God's spoken word.

Again, what was I thinking? I felt good about the prayer and ended with an "Amen." When I looked up, Sarah's eyes were filled with tears and she had a look of terror on her face. My first reaction, "What's wrong?" was followed by, "What could have happened? We were praying! Prayers are good things. Prayers should make us happy and calm our fears." Sarah began to bawl as she expressed her fear of Satan "prowling around like a roaring lion" coming to get her. Oh boy! Next time, I'll use the child-friendly version of scriptures.

AM I A GOOD MOM?

Train up a child in the way he should go, and when he
is old he will not depart from it. Proverbs 22:6 (NKJV)

Being a parent is hard! These unique little souls don't come with
individualized owner's manuals. Our responsibilities are numerous
and sometimes overwhelming; besides feeding them, clothing them,
educating them, keeping them safe, nurturing them, monitoring their
emotional well-being and spiritual growth, we are faced with the task
of figuring out how to discipline these little munchkins who eventually
turn into big munchkins. Raising our children in church and applying
consistent discipline at home often doesn't seem enough. We cover them
daily with prayers, and hope their behavior at home and at school is
appropriate. Unfortunately, we cannot control our children's behavior
every single minute of the day, and when their choices do not reflect
the godly precepts we have taught them at home, we tend to question
ourselves and our parenting skills.

Sarah and Sophie met James, a little boy in their kindergarten class,
and all three of them became fast friends. James was absolutely adorable

with his whitish blond hair, big blue eyes, and the biggest smile ever! James loved my girls and they loved him, too. Actually, I think he was *in love* with Sarah. He often tried to kiss her, but she rebuffed his affection.

One afternoon when I picked the girls up from school, Sophie began telling me the story about James kicking her in the shin while they were playing during recess. I probably overreacted by uttering a loud, "What? What do you mean James kicked you? Why would he kick you? What did you do to him?" Sophie adamantly responded, "Mom, I didn't do anything to him! He just kicked me!" Well, I knew better than that, James was not a mean kid nor a bully, and he wouldn't walk over to Sophie or Sarah and kick them without a reason. That's when Sarah piped in, "It's because she kicked him out of the Wolf Pack." Now I understood, James was mad because Sophie kicked him out of the Wolf Pack, so in response to his ejection from the group, he kicked Sophie. Or at least I thought I had the story right, so I repeated it verbatim to make sure I had all the facts.

The truth was James kicked Sophie for no obvious reason, so in turn she kicked him out of the Wolf Pack, not the other way around. Either way I knew that James was a good boy, but I felt the need to take a picture of the bruise and send it to his mother. James' mother, Sara, and I became friends when the kids met in kindergarten, so I felt comfortable tattle telling on James. Sara is very reasonable, and old school like me; she's raising her children in a Christian home with traditional values which consists of knowing right from wrong, and she will discipline them appropriately while taking the opportunity to turn the incident into a teachable moment.

When Sara found out what James did, she was horrified and responded, "I didn't hear anything about this! I will be sure and talk to him. He absolutely loves Sophie and knows better than to hit or kick anyone! I'm so sorry but please know I will get to the bottom of it." She made James write lines, "I will not kick my friends," twenty-five times. James also wrote an apology letter (on a big red heart) and gave it to Sophie the following day at school. Sophie was over the situation by the next day, back to being friends with James, and eventually let him back into the Wolf Pack. She has such a sweet and forgiving heart; I admire that trait in her.

Several days later, Sara and I talked on the phone. She informed me that James had been having trouble at school. Not only had he kicked Sophie; he had also punched another little girl in their class, in the face. His behavior was getting him into trouble, and she didn't know why. I could tell as she talked, she was frustrated and was doing everything she knew to do to help her son. She explained that she questioned James about being bullied, but he denied that anyone was bullying him. Even Sarah and Sophie were adamant that no one at school was bullying James, but something was said about his hair and his glasses.

I could tell that Sara's heart was breaking for her child, and she felt desperate for answers. She and her husband decided to take James for testing to get to the bottom of his unexplained aggression. I wanted Sara to know that I wasn't mad at James, or at her, for what happened, I just wanted her to be aware of the situation. I could tell she was trying to hold back tears, but her voice cracked under the weight of her emotions and exposed her. She asked the one question that every mother secretly asks herself day in and day out when the rough times hit and chaos consumes our families, and we plead urgently with God to calm the storm, "Am I a good mom?" I've asked myself that same question a thousand times. If you ask my children, they will reply with a resounding, "Yes!" If you ask other people in my family, the ones who tend to be judgmental and criticize everything I do that is different from the way they raised their children, the answer is probably, "It's questionable". Thank the good Lord for my sweet mama who reassures me from time to time that, "Yes, in fact I am a good mom." It's nice to hear those words from others who understand the trials and tribulations only moms experience. So, I reassured Sara that indeed she was a good mom; I told her that the fact that she worried about being a good mom was evidence that she was, *in fact*, a good mom! She thanked me, saying she really needed to hear that. We all do. If you are seeking the Lord's wisdom and guidance as you raise your children, your daughters, you are already ahead of the game.

Continue On by Roy Lessin is an amazing poem highlighting the roles that women play as wives and mothers, and how God sees everything that we do. I'll paraphrase my interpretation of the poem:

As women, wives, and mothers we often wonder about the usefulness of our lives. Are we wasting our true potential? Mothers invest a lot of time into their husbands and children, but often feel discouraged because they are unappreciated. Scriptures tell us that God sees and hears us. So, as we continue on in our roles as mothers and wives, we can take heart in knowing that God is our reward. Our service to our family and our obedience to God greatly pleases Him.

*Please visit _www.meetinginthemeadow.com_ to read Mr. Lessin's poem in its entirety.

> Sometimes we can get "down in the dumps" and begin
> to question God's calling on our lives. The struggle to
> do all and to be all, is real. Scripture urges, "Let us not
> become weary in doing good, for at the proper time we
> will reap a harvest if we do not give up".
>
> Galatians 6:9 (NIV)

BEING A ROLE MODEL

Our pastor decided that he wanted to start 2021 off with prayer and fasting, so he asked our congregation to join him in a twenty-one day fast, starting in January. He wanted us to corporately do this so that we could collectively hear from the Lord regarding His plans for our church in the upcoming year. It had been a while since I had fasted, so I knew that it would definitely be a sacrifice. 2020 had been a hectic year and I was suffering the consequences of my gluttony, brain fog and an extra ten pounds. Fasting would be a terrific way to spend more time reading my Bible and praying while listening for God's voice; it was also a great diet plan, so I made the commitment in my heart, and purposed that I would fast from sugar and sweets for twenty-one days.

The Friday prior to this fasting commitment, Sarah had asked me to bake some Monster Cookies, our family's favorite cookies. I have been baking these cookies for twenty years and everyone loves them. Everyone I know personally, or who I've worked with, or gone to church or Bible study with, or is my neighbor, or have gone to school with my kids, have tasted these famous Monster Cookies. I have yet to find someone who doesn't like them. Don't worry, you won't be left out; I'll put the recipe at the end of this chapter for everyone to enjoy.

No judgment please, but I let Sarah and Sophie eat Monster Cookies for breakfast. They are healthier than most breakfast foods because they have oatmeal (whole grains), peanut butter (protein), chocolate chips (which contain antioxidants), and a few other ingredients which I won't mention right now. But I can attest to the fact they are not purely sugar, like cinnamon rolls, a cheese Danish, or Fruity Pebbles. And of course, I let them drink a glass of white milk (calcium) with their cookies.

One morning I began fixing the girls their breakfast, which consisted of warmed Monster Cookies and a tall glass white milk. While rifling through the cookie jar searching for the most perfectly formed round cookies, I pinched off a small piece and put it in my mouth... Instantly I gasped, "Oh no!" as my eyes widened and I clasped my hand over my mouth. I hadn't even attempted to chew when I realized what I had done. How is it that only five minutes earlier, I had disavowed sugar and sweets and committed to fasting?

Now I was standing in my kitchen trying to decide what to do about my predicament. What should I do, spit it out, or just swallow it and ask for forgiveness?" You don't understand, Monster Cookies are the Holy Grail in our family. A hot commodity. You don't just spit them out or throw them away, that would be sacrilegious, and wasteful! But I had made a commitment to God and my children were watching me. Well, I did the right thing and spit out the piece I so mindlessly put into my mouth. How quickly we forget the promises, vows, and covenants that we make with our God.

I knew fasting would be challenging, because temptations are everywhere, but I had faith that with the help of the Holy Spirit, I could do it! Several months before Sarah and Sophie's eighth birthday, I promised I would take them to the Galleria in Houston to go ice skating as part of their birthday present. We invited their friend Harper and her mom, Holly. Our plans consisted of ice skating, possibly a little shopping, and lunch at The Cheesecake Factory, of course. They have the best, most delicious Lemon Raspberry Cream cheesecake. I daydreamed about enjoying one piece, guilt free, while at the Galleria.

It dawned on me about a week before our trip to Houston, that I had committed to fasting and prayer for twenty-one days; I still had one more week to go. How was I going to enjoy a piece of cheesecake, if I was fasting from sugar and sweets? I don't go to Houston that often, so when I eat at the Cheesecake Factory it's always a treat. I knew what I would have to do, pass on the cheesecake, but I went to one of my co-workers for advice. After I explained my dilemma, she jokingly suggested, "Maybe they have sugar free cheesecake."

Loopholes, our sinful nature is always looking for loopholes. How could I have that delicious piece of creamy, luscious, heavenly Lemon Raspberry cheesecake without breaking my fasting vow to God? The truth is I couldn't, because I'm fully aware that little eyes are watching me all of the time. How we as mothers act and react to circumstances, becomes our daughters' examples to follow. The "do as I say, not as I do" rhetoric does not work. They will mimic my behaviors or follow in my footsteps observing everything I do. I must purposely be the *role model* that they need, modeling behaviors, habits, and attitudes I want them to emulate.

I have yelled, I have cried, I have given in, and more often than not, I have demonstrated many wrong behaviors. For that, I have had to humble myself and apologize to my daughters many times for overreacting or losing my cool. Their sweet, forgiving, precious hearts always accept my apology, and our encounters always end with a hug, a kiss, and "I love you!" I'm grateful that Sarah and Sophie never hold a grudge or stay mad at me for long.

As mothers, we need to speak God's word over our daughters, as well as guide them in their studies of the Scriptures. We also need to be role models for our daughters, which is an arduous task because we are flawed, imperfect humans; ones that inadvertently sin in front of our audience of offspring. This is when we need to call upon the Lord for strength and wisdom, to be that role model for the next generation of daughters.

Parenting is hard, but it's not about being perfect, it's about being consistent. I'm imperfect and have fallen short of God's glory as a parent, but each new day He offers me grace and mercy to continue on in this extraordinary journey as Sarah and Sophie's mom. May I never take this calling for granted.

Monster Cookies

1 stick of butter softened (HEB brand salted stick butter)
1 ½ cup of smooth peanut butter (Peter Pan)
1 cup dark brown sugar (Imperial)
1 cup of white sugar (Imperial)
3 eggs (Cage-free brown - size large)
1 tsp. vanilla (Pure vanilla extract, not imitation)
2 tsp. baking soda (Arm & Hammer)
1 lb. bag chocolate chips (Nestle Toll House semi sweet)
4 ½ cups oatmeal (Quaker brand One Minute Oats)

Mix the ingredients together in the order they appear on the recipe, adding one ingredient at a time. Add your chocolate chips first and then add one cup at a time of oatmeal until you've added 4 ½ cups. Using an ice cream scoop (for large cookies) or a melon baller (for smaller cookies) drop batter onto parchment lined cookie sheets. Bake for 12 minutes at 350 degrees.

9

BE BOLD LIKE QUEEN ESTHER

I was one of those students who always received *checks in the third column* for talking too much. I couldn't help it; I liked to talk, and I had a lot to say. Let me share a few stories with you. My freshman year in high school, I ended up in Mr. Tolar's Earth Science class with two of my very best friends, Amy and Rondell. Yes, this is the same Amy I mentioned in a previous chapter who I twirled with in middle school.

Our classroom was set up with tables that sat four students each all facing the front board. Of course, Amy, Rondell, and I sat together; how could we not? We had so much to discuss: boys, relationships, and extracurricular activities. Amy sat at one end of the table to my right, I sat in the middle, Rondell sat on the other side of me to my left, and poor Casey Sauer sat at the other end of the table.

Every single day during class we'd visit and pass notes to each other because we didn't have enough time during transition between classes, to chat and catch up on the latest gossip or current events. You know for high school girls socializing is the epitome of their existence. Spending time with your friends and making sure you get those 20,000 words-a-day in, is paramount. So, back and forth, back and forth we'd talk. Because I sat between Amy and Rondell, my attention would shift from one to the other. Eventually, our teacher had had enough, decided to separate us, and move us to opposite ends of the classroom. He said I looked like I was watching a tennis match, because I would look to my right at Amy and then to my left at Rondell. I guess I hadn't really thought about how distracting my behavior may have been to him and other students in my class. I knew I was talking too much, but I was just being me. I will say I was slightly embarrassed when he moved me. Did I mention he was also my Sunday School teacher that year?

Not only do I talk too much, but I also talk too fast. I guess I'm making sure I get every word in before someone butts into my conversation and cuts me off. One semester while I was at Texas A&M my aunt and uncle, who lived in Houston, invited me down for the weekend. They enticed me with a home cooked meal and free access to a washer and dryer, instead of having to spend all my quarters on washing my clothes at the laundromat. My aunt cooked spaghetti with mushrooms and meatballs, made a fresh salad, and baked garlic bread. I didn't cook at all in college, so I truly appreciated this meal. I shared with my family all the exciting activities I was involved in at A&M, telling them about new friends I had made, and of course, bragging on our Aggie football and baseball teams. They were good listeners and let me talk through the entire meal. Finally, my Uncle Billy reached over and put his hand on my arm, leaned toward me and said, "We're not going anywhere Stephanie, you can slow down. You don't have to talk so fast," then he grinned and let out a little laugh while shaking his head back and forth. As I mentioned earlier, I was just being me.

In my early twenties, I sought out a Christian counselor for some guidance and advice because I was going through a difficult time. He encouraged me to spend time in prayer, read a few Christian self-help books, and engage in some introspection. I had recently graduated from college and my life wasn't going according to *my* plan. I didn't have a job, and honestly didn't know what I wanted to do, or how I would use my seemingly useless psychology degree.

Unlike most of my girlfriends, I hadn't met my future husband yet either, which was quite distressing to me. I began to question God about my future and any possible reasons *why* I was still single. Maybe I hadn't found the right person, maybe I was too picky, or maybe there was something wrong with me? Did it have something to do with my personality? Whatever the reason, I was unhappy and in a rut, stuck, not knowing how to deal with my feelings.

Sometimes you don't realize how others perceive you, your actions, or your words until someone points these idiosyncrasies out; for instance, at the conclusion of our first session, my counselor prayed with me and asked God to "Give [me] the Spirit of wisdom and revelation, so that [I] may know him better. I pray that the eyes of your heart may be enlightened in order that you may know the hope to which he has called you, the riches of his glorious inheritance in his holy people." His prayer and the scripture he quoted comforted me and I exhaled a sigh of relief believing everything was going to be alright. Then he added, "Don't worry, in time, we'll round off some of those *rough edges.*" Record scratch! "Rough edges," what was he talking about? I didn't know that I had rough edges. At one time or another I might have put a few people *in their place*, but I was only reacting to *their* words or behavior. I might have confidently and enthusiastically stated my opinion once or twice. But rough edges, really? My parents never pointed out those *rough edges*, nor anyone in my family, nor my Sunday School teacher, nor friends, nor neighbors. What a revelation! Talk about being oblivious to my lack of self-awareness. He pointed out that people *like me* are often perceived as rude, harsh, unkind, lacking empathy and often end up offending others. Well, I never meant to offend anyone, I was only being honest; the Bible does tell us to "speak the truth!"

So, I began praying about these *rough edges* and hoped God would smooth them all out, through *the washing of the word*; the process is still on-going. I believe it's better to acknowledge our faults and learn our lessons early on because, "The fear of the Lord is the beginning of wisdom and knowledge of the Holy One is understanding," Proverbs 9:10 (NIV) and I want all of the wisdom and understanding I can get!

During one conversation with God, I was complaining to Him and telling Him I really didn't like my personality. I have always envied those girls in school who were "the most popular"; they were laid back and easy going, friendly to everyone, they had the most friends, and they always appeared to be happy and smiling. Everyone liked these girls who were always voted "most popular" of their class, for student council or Homecoming Court, Miss Congeniality during CavOilcade, and dated the cutest most popular boys. And that was all during high school. What about those girls in sororities, the Diamond Darlings of the baseball team, or the girls who found their prince charming in college, got married after graduation, and lived happily ever after? I really wanted to be like them, but I wasn't. Why did God make me this way? Clearly and plainly God said to me, "You have the personality of Queen Esther." I responded, "Queen Esther?" [Now mind you, I'm having this conversation with God out loud as I'm walking out of Dillard's through the parking lot of Parkdale Mall to my car.]

I didn't know much about Esther, but the fact that she was a queen, momentarily gave me comfort. And I'd like to mention that my name, Stephanie, means *crowned one*. So, how bad could I be if I was like one of the queens mentioned in the Bible? One who even has an entire chapter in the Bible named after her? I drove home as fast as I could; hopeful enthusiasm mounting as I opened my Bible to the book of Esther. I began reading and asking God to show me the traits that I shared with Esther because I desperately needed reassurance that the traits God had woven into my personality weren't all that bad. God revealed to me that because of Queen Esther's great faith and boldness, she made a decision that could have meant life or death for her and her people.

We are introduced to Esther in the book of Esther, in Chapter 2, verse 7; she is a young, beautiful virgin with a lovely figure. She is sent to King Xerxes's palace, by her cousin Mordecai, who raised her as his own because she was an orphan. King Xerxes has banished his queen, Vashti, and is looking for a new queen to take her place. Because of Esther's beauty, Mordecai believes that the King will be pleased with her, and she might have the chance to become the new queen. Mordecai forbids Esther to reveal her nationality and family background at that time.

Traditionally, Esther along with many other young women, would go in front of the King, and if he was pleased with one of them, he would summon her by name. "Now the King was attracted to Esther more than any of the other women, and she won his favor and approval more than any of the other virgins. So he [King Xerxes] set a royal crown on her head and made her queen instead of Vashti. And the king gave a great banquet, Esther's banquet, for all his nobles and officials."

Then the drama began when King Xerxes chose to honor a man named Haman, who presided within the King's court. "Everyone bowed down to him (or paid him honor), except Mordecai, because Mordecai was a Jew like Esther. Mordecai's refusal to bow down, enraged Haman to the point that he vows to 'destroy Mordecai and his people, throughout the whole kingdom of Xerxes.'"

Haman sent out a decree ordering all Jews to be "destroyed, killed, and annihilated." When Mordecai heard this, he tore his clothes and covered himself with ashes and was very distressed. Queen Esther inquired about Mordecai's behavior; he told her the whole story and begged her to go into the King's presence to beg for mercy and plead with him for their people [her people].

Royal protocol at that time, forbad anyone to come before the King except if they were summoned. "Mordecai said to Esther, 'Do not think that because you are in the King's house you alone of all the Jews, will escape. For if you remain silent at this time, relief and deliverance from the Jews will arise from another place, but you and your family will perish. And who knows but that you have come to your royal position for 'such a time as this'"? Esther agreed to do as Mordecai asked and responded with absolute resolve, "If I perish, I perish."

So, Esther dressed in her finest robe and went to see King Xerxes. When he saw Queen Esther standing in the court, he was pleased with her and held out to her the golden scepter that was in his hand. She petitioned the King, "Grant me my life and spare my people." Fortunately, King Xerxes granted Queen Esther her petition and drew up a new "edict, granting the Jews in every city the right to assemble and protect themselves and to destroy, kill, and annihilate the armed men of any nationality or province who might attack them and their women and children."

I share this story from the Bible because Esther was a real person, who lived and breathed, and walked upon this earth, just like you and me. She wasn't superhuman or special in any way, until God chose to use her to save the Jewish people, her people, God's people. She knowingly and boldly chose to break tradition and protocol and go into the King's presence without being summoned. I'm sure she was afraid and uncertain of the outcome, but she did what she had to do. She is an example to me, to my daughters, and to other women who face difficult circumstances, when only our faith and boldness will bring life, and a peaceful resolution.

I am thankful God thinks so highly of me, to liken me to Queen Esther, such a kinship makes me feel special. It helps me to see I have a purpose here on earth, "To boldly make known the mystery of the Gospel." I want to be bold like her, not just one time, but time and time again. I want my daughters to be bold like Queen Esther too, even if their choices end up being sacrificial but for the greater good of others, because I know God will protect them and bless them. I'm beginning to realize that God is using me and my big mouth to speak to His people words of truth and encouragement. Thank the good Lord above for insight, wisdom, and His Word to help me navigate this road to understanding how and why he made me the way I am, and what purpose He had in creating me. I realized that God will use my lips, my voice, and my words to share my testimony with others. So maybe talking too much isn't such a bad thing?

What I want Sarah and Sophie to learn from this lesson is, their words are powerful and have enormous influence over others; their words can uplift and encourage or tear down and destroy. I want them to realize that how they speak to others is also a reflection of the condition of their heart. I want them to be more introspective than I was as a teenager and young adult. I want Sarah and Sophie to know their giftings, passions, vocation, and purpose for their lives. To live their lives knowing God has a purpose and a plan for each one of them, so they won't spend years wandering around aimlessly wasting time wondering why they are here on this earth and what role God wants them to have in his kingdom; to walk out their destiny with resolve to be obedient to the Lord, to fulfill His calling on their lives, and to touch as many lives as possible for the Gospel and His glory. Amen!

> The Lord announces the Word, and the women who proclaim it are a mighty throng.
>
> Psalm 68:11 (NIV)

I have one more itty, bitty, little thing to confess; I still struggle with *speaking the truth in love*. In Ephesians 4:15 we are admonished to "speak the truth in love." As I mentioned earlier, I have absolutely no problem speaking my mind and telling others what I think regardless of whether my input is solicited or not; however, this approach comes off as abrasive, tends to offend people, and typically doesn't work well in drawing the unsaved to Jesus. That is why God has given us [me] his Word so, we know how we should speak to one another especially when the truth is hard to hear. I have to stay in the Word and under the guidance of the Holy Spirit to keep myself and my words in-check.

Thank the good Lord that I'm still a work in progress, His grace is sufficient, and His mercies are new every morning. And I know that I'll get another chance to speak the truth to others in love, with kindness, compassion, and understanding.

> Instead, speaking the truth in love, we will grow to become in every respect the mature body of him who is the head, that is, Christ.
>
> Ephesians 4:15 (NIV)

THE ARMOR OF GOD

Empowering our daughters with the Word of God to fight the good fight.

> Fight the good fight of the faith. Take hold of the eternal life to which you were called when you made your good confession in the presence of many witnesses.
> 1 Timothy 6:12 (NIV)

I've talked a lot about God's Word in previous chapters; teaching our daughters the Word of God is important, encouraging them to hide God's Word deep in their hearts is key to their understanding of God and His character. Our daughters must understand the accurate nature of God: He is loving, faithful, and merciful and He gave us His Word to "teach, rebuke, correct and train us in righteousness." His Word equips us for our lifelong journey here on earth.

The Spiritual War

For though we walk in the flesh, we do not war according to the flesh. For the weapons of our warfare are not carnal but mighty in God for pulling down strongholds, casting down arguments and every high thing that exalts itself against the knowledge of God, bringing every thought into captivity to the obedience of Christ... 2 Corinthians 10:3-5 (NKJV)

Finally, be strong in the Lord and in his mighty power. Put on the full armor of God, so that you can take your stand against the devil's schemes. For our struggle is not against flesh and blood, but against the rulers, against the authorities, against the powers of this dark world and against the spiritual forces of evil in the heavenly realms. Ephesians 6:10-12 (NIV)

Another version states, "For we do not wrestle against flesh and blood, but against principalities, against powers, against rulers of the darkness of this age, against spiritual hosts of wickedness in the heavenly places. Therefore, take up the whole armor of God, that you may be able to withstand in the evil day, and having done all, to stand." (NKJV)

But my very favorite translation of this scripture is from The Passion Translation, "Put on God's complete set of armor provided for us, so that you will be protected as you fight against the evil strategies of the accuser! Your hand-to-hand combat is not with human beings, but with the highest principalities and authorities operating in rebellion under the heavenly realms. For they are a powerful class of demon-gods and evil spirits that hold this dark world in bondage. Because of this, you must wear all the armor that God provides so you're protected as you confront the slanderer, for you are destined for all things and will rise victorious."

Whether we want to admit it or not, there is war being waged daily for our precious daughters' souls. God, our amazing creator, wants us to believe His Word, and in His son, Jesus Christ. God wants us to "know the truth, and the truth will set you free" John 8:32 (NIV). The enemy of our hearts is Satan, and the spiritual battle is real! If our daughters do not know the Word of God, then how can they "fight the good fight of the faith" and be victorious? The Bible tells us that "The thief [Satan] comes only to steal and kill and destroy; I [Jesus] have come that you may have life and have it to the full" John 10:10 (NIV). The responsibility is ours, parents, guardians, and the body of Christ to teach our daughters God's Word, so that they will be successful in their battles. When warring against the wiles of the devil, God's Word can be used in two ways; it can protect us from his attacks and it can slay the lies of the enemy, who seeks to deceive and destroy our daughters. Teaching our daughters to put on the full armor of God daily, will protect them from the schemes of the devil.

Therefore, take up the full armor of God, that you may be able to withstand in the evil day, and having done all, to stand. Ephesians 6:13 (NKJV)

I memorized this scripture during the two years I waited for God to fulfill his promise to me for a mate. I struggled to wait on the Lord for my future husband. Satan was relentless in his attacks on my mind. Negative thoughts bombarded my thinking daily, even hourly as I struggled to believe God's Word and His promises to me. Often Satan used people to discourage me to give up on my dream and on God's promises. Reading my Bible daily and memorizing scripture was the only thing I knew to do, to fight against these incessant attacks by Satan. I wrote Ephesians 6:14-19 on an index card and taped it to my mirror, so that I would see it every morning when I put on my makeup, i.e., warpaint.

> Stand therefore, having girded your waist with the truth, having put on the breastplate of righteousness, and having shod your feet with the preparation of the gospel of peace; above all, taking the shield of faith with which, you will be able to quench all the fiery darts of the wicked one. And take the helmet of salvation, and the sword of the Spirit, which is the Word of God; praying always with all prayer and supplication in the Spirit, being watchful to this end with all perseverance and supplication for all the saints. Ephesians 6:14-18 (NKJV)

This may sound silly, but I rehearsed this scripture every morning going through the motions of putting on every piece of the armor of God. I knew that on those days when I was feeling weak, I needed His protection from the on-going harassment of the devil. My mind, my circumstances, my family and friends, and the world were all telling me that I was insane to believe what God had spoken to me. How could I possibly marry a man that I wasn't dating or even speaking to, much less, hadn't spoken to in over a year? Ridiculous, I know! But when God has promised you something and you know with every fiber of your being that what God said is true, the devil will do everything in his power to discourage you from holding on to that promise. He doesn't want you to be victorious, but you must battle through to the end, to the fulfillment of *the promise*, then you will stand victorious holding *the promise* in your hand. Whatever the promise may be, a husband, a baby, a new job, a new house, a sober family member, a restored relationship, salvation for lost souls. You will be victorious because God's promises are true, and His word never returns void.

The Armor of God

1. Belt of Truth
2. Breastplate of Righteousness
3. Gospel of Peace
4. Shield of Faith
5. Helmet of Salvation
6. Sword of the Spirit (Word of God)

Notice five of the pieces of armor are defensive in nature, each piece protects us from the enemy's attacks. The only piece of armor used as a weapon offensively is the Sword of the Spirit, which is the Word of God.

At the beginning of this passage of scripture, starting with verse 13 we are told, "Therefore put on the full armor of God, so that when the day of evil comes, you may be able to stand your ground, and after you have done everything, to stand." What does it mean to stand?

There are many varying dictionary definitions of the word *stand,* so I chose three that helped me to understand this passage. 1. to remain stationary, 2. having or maintaining an upright position, and 3. an act of holding one's ground against or halting to resist an opposing force. My understanding of this passage, supported by other scriptures, leads me to believe, once we put on the full armor of God, we have done our part as commanded in the scripture, then we are ready to *stand* prepared for any attacks hurled our way.

This is the very reason I've (Paul) been made a minister by the authority of God and a servant to his body, so that in his detailed plan I would fully equip you with the Word of God! Colossians 1:25 (TPT) As mothers, this is also part of our ministry to our daughters, making sure they are equipped with the Word of God.

At the end of the passage in Ephesians 6, after naming all of the pieces of God's armor, most people stop at verse 18, but when I memorized this scripture long ago, I always included verse 19 which says, "and for me, that utterance may be given to me, that I may open my mouth *boldly* to make known the mystery of the gospel." As I mentioned earlier in this book, I believe that my spiritual gift is prophecy. Several times in my life, during a simple conversation I have prophesied to the person I was speaking with. Oftentimes, God puts the right words in my mouth, to minister to that person. Several times, I have had the person ask me to repeat what I've just said, but I can't because it was God who was speaking, not I. This is one of the mysteries verse 19 is speaking of.

The gospel of Jesus Christ has many mysteries that our finite minds cannot comprehend; it is only through our faith and active role the Holy Spirit plays in our lives, that will allow us to use those giftings. I also mentioned earlier in this book that I believed God told me that I had the personality of Queen Esther, who was unbelievably bold. She risked her own life to save her people when she boldly entered the King's chamber uninvited. If the King had been displeased with her actions, he could have had her killed right on the spot; however, God went before her and prepared the King's heart to hear her pleas for her people.

Talk about bold. I'm not sure if I would have had the confidence to do what Queen Esther did, but I hope that I walk daily in the confidence to speak God's truth into people's lives.

In the preceding paragraph I stated that it is only with the supernatural help of the Holy Spirit that we can speak truth and speak God's Word boldly. In the book of Acts, Chapter 4, we read about the imparting of the Holy Spirit after Peter and John pray. "At that moment the earth shook beneath them, causing the building they were in to tremble. Each one of them was filled with the Holy Spirit, and they proclaimed the Word of God with *unrestrained boldness*" Act. 4:31 (TPT). I believe my life is a testimony for others to see that God's Word is true and that it works. All because I trust Him daily as I put on the armor of God, and He gives me the boldness to continue telling my story.

Incorporating scripture into my writing is a form of prophesying. We know that "all scripture is God-breathed" 2 Timothy 3:16 (NIV). "In the beginning was the Word, and the Word was with God, and the Word was God" John 1:1 (NIV). God's word "does not return void" Isaiah 55:11 (NKJV). God's word is "living and active" Hebrews 4:12 (ESV). Therefore, when we speak God's Word over our daughters, we can rest assured knowing that they are ensconced in the protected refuge of His loving wings.

He shall cover you with His feathers, And under His wings you shall take refuge; His truth shall be your shield and buckler. Psalm 91:4 (NKJV)

As a mother, I can breathe a sigh of relief and rest assured that my daughters are protected daily; I will do my part and pray for them, they will have to do their part and put on the full armor of God, and God will do His part.

Two immensely powerful ways to use God's Word as a weapon to fight against the devil's wiles are praise and worship. In Psalm 149:6-7 (TPT) David talks about the power of praising God. "God's high and holy praise fill their mouths, for their shouted praises are their weapons of war! These warring weapons will bring vengeance on every opposing force and every resistant power." In Psalms 18:34, 39, 43 David says to God, "You've trained me with the weapons of warfare-worship; now I'll descend down into battle with power to chase and conquer my foes. You empower me for victory with your wrap-around presence. You've placed your armor upon me…You gave me victory on every side…"

The order in which you put on your armor doesn't really matter. Just make sure you put on each piece daily, so that you are equipped to go out into this world prepared for the battle (spiritual).

One of my favorite songs that speaks of spiritual warfare and victory is "**Victory**" by Yolanda Adams. The scripture in Psalm 20:4-5 (TPT) closely parallels the lyrics of her song. "May God give you every desire of your heart and carry out your every plan as you go to battle. When you succeed, we will celebrate and shout for you. Flags will fly when victory is yours! Yes, God will answer your prayers and we will praise him." I have included some lines from her song to reiterate my belief that God will give you *the victory* every single time.

Victory

By Yolanda Adams

I've fought many, many battles in his name/
I held up the blood-stained banner/
And proclaimed that Jesus is the truth and the light/
Believe me when I say he will make it right/

Chorus:
I've got, got the victory/
I've got the sweet, sweet victory in Jesus/
He is a mighty conqueror/
In him I will trust all my battles he'll fight.

DESTINY

It is the Lord who directs your life, for each step you take is ordained by God to bring you closer to your destiny. So much of your life then, remains a mystery!

Proverbs 20:24 (TPT)

Because I have struggled with walking in my own destiny, I don't want Sarah and Sophie to struggle as I have. Many prayers have been prayed for them since they were wee babies, to know what their passions are at an early age. To seek out those interests that intrigue them, and to continually make wise choices that propel each one of them into the future and calling that God has placed upon their lives.

In Psalm 139:1-10, 13-16 (NIV) King David speaks of God's intimate knowledge of each and every one of us.

You have searched me, LORD, and you know me. You know when I sit and when I rise; you perceive my thoughts from afar. You discern my going out and my lying down; you are familiar with all my ways. Before a word is on my tongue, you, LORD, know it completely. You hem me in behind and before, and you lay your hand upon me. Such knowledge is too wonderful for me, too lofty for me to attain. Where can I go from your Spirit? Where can I flee from your presence? If I go up to the heavens, you are there; if I make my bed in the depths, you are there. If I rise on the wings of the dawn, if I settle on the far side of the sea, even there your hand will guide me, your right hand will hold me fast (v. 1-10). For you created my inmost being; you knit me together in my mother's womb. I praise you because I am fearfully and wonderfully made; your works are wonderful; I know that full well. My frame was not hidden from you when I was made in the secret place, when I was woven together in the depths of the earth. Your eyes saw my unformed body; **all the days ordained for me were written in your book before one of them came to be** (v. 13-16).

How exciting to know that God has already ordained our daughters' steps, so as they grow, mature, and develop, they will walk the path God has already paved for them. As a mom, such news gives me great comfort knowing that I don't have to worry or fret; God's got this.

Life entails so many unknowns, and as human nature would have it, we tend to struggle with the *not knowing* part. Mothers often like to control the environment that surrounds their children because we want them to be safe. We want to guide them because *it is our job*. We want to make sure they have everything they need physically, emotionally, and spiritually to succeed in life, and as I'm slowly figuring out, our daughters have to be willing participants in these life-learning processes. I want what's best for my girls, but more than that, I want God's best for them.

Oftentimes, parents have preconceived notions of what they want their children to accomplish in life, starting at a young age. Just from my observations, I see parents reliving their lives through their children, their children's activities, and their children's accomplishments. I guess I don't understand the concept of "living through your children" because I did everything I wanted to do while growing up. My time has come and gone and I'm okay with that.

Whatever activities my children choose to be involved in, the idea originated within themselves, not me. I've made numerous suggestions about activities I thought my girls would enjoy participating in, but to my chagrin, they tell me "No" more often than not, and I'm not of the school of thought to force my children to do things they have absolutely no interest in. So, I'll "leave my [daughters'] destiny and its timing in [the Lord's] your hands" Psalm 16:5 (TPT).

When Sarah and Sophie were younger, there wasn't any conflict between us about attending baking camp at Rao's, swimming lessons with Ms. Maria, VBS, cheer camp, or jiu-jitsu; they enjoyed every activity I signed them up for. Now, there's a battle every Tuesday when I tell Sarah to get dressed for gymnastics. She used to love going to gymnastics, but the harder the skills became the more effort she had to exert, and she's just not about that. I'm not insinuating she's lazy, but for whatever reason, she lacks confidence in performing some of the skills without having an instructor standing by to spot her.

Sophie, on the other hand, has no problem with confidence. At the age of five, she started jiu-jitsu and absolutely loved it. She looked so cute in her little white Gi. She grappled with girls and boys who had more experience than she did, and she never backed down. She thought jiu-jitsu would help her to be a better police officer and beat the bad guys up. I explained to her that police officers don't beat up their suspects, and jiu-jitsu is not an offensive sport, but a defensive sport. Regardless of my explanations, she continued on with jiu-jitsu until she moved on to soccer, which she also loves. This Mommie doesn't like sitting out in the freezing cold or the blistering heat, but I do it for her.

The push these days is for children to be involved in every extracurricular activity under the sun: little league baseball, basketball, flag-football, dance, gymnastics, you name it. My husband and I agree that our girls only need to be involved in one extracurricular activity each semester because family life and attending church are our first priorities.

In Psalm 25:9-10 (TPT) the scripture so beautifully tells us, "Keep showing the humble your path, and lead them into the best decision. Bring revelation light that trains them in the truth. May they obey you and follow you in the pleasant paths of love and faithfulness! For your love surrounds them as your truth takes them forward." Thank you, Lord that I don't have to worry about my daughters and their future, as long as I keep doing my job as a mother and teaching them about God's character and His amazing love for them, He will take care of the rest.

Before I formed you in the womb I knew you, before you were born I set you apart. Jeremiah 1:5 (NIV)

I am sure you've heard the name Jennifer Hudson; in 2004 she competed in the 3rd season of American Idol finishing in seventh place. Jennifer was a powerful singer and received rave reviews from the judges; many people thought she would win first place. After one of her final dynamic performances, one of the judges confidently stated, "Let me sum this up for you. I think you're out of your depth. There are people better than you and I don't think you can do anything better to have any chance of ever winning this competition." Jennifer was quite shocked at this critique and the perplexed look on her face showed. The aforementioned judge is a professional music producer who carries the power in the music industry to *make or break* struggling artists' careers; his stunning evaluation of Jennifer's performances and singing ability was limited to his short-sightedness and human perspective, or should I say, "his opinion."

In 2006, Jennifer made her film debut as Effie White in the film adaptation of the Broadway musical, *Dream Girls,* for which she won the Academy Award for Best Supporting Actress becoming the youngest African American to win in a competitive acting category. Then in 2008, she signed with Arista Records and released her self-titled debut studio album, which was certified gold, sold over a million copies, and won the Grammy award for Best R&B Album. She, along with the cast of the Broadway revival of *The Color Purple,* won the 2016 Tony award for Best Revival.

What if Jennifer would have believed that one judge's discouraging, pessimistic critique? What if she had taken his words to heart, as truth? How different her life would have been if she would have walked away from her passion and God-given talent?

As she graciously accepted her Oscar for winning Best Supporting Actress, the first words she uttered were, "Look what God can do!" She thanked others for helping her, thanked God again, and ended her speech saying, "Thank you for helping me keep the faith, even when I didn't believe."

I am thankful Jennifer didn't walk away from her dreams, and remained steadfast and determined because the world would not have been blessed by her beautiful voice and story of triumph. God had a plan for Jennifer Hudson, a destiny to fulfill, and she continues to have success as she walks out her destiny. God always has the final say and no human can thwart His plans.

> We have become his poetry, a re-created people that will fulfill the destiny he has given each of us, for we are joined to Jesus, the Anointed One. Even before we were born, God planned in advance our destiny and the good works we would do to fulfill it! Ephesians 2:10 (TPT)

True success is knowing your worth in the eyes of God and using your gifts.

—Jentezen Franklin, author

As we live our lives, as our daughters live their lives, they will be the example of never-ending pursuit, hard work, and remaining faithful to their dreams and goals believing what God spoke to them concerning their future and destiny. "May he work perfection into every part of you [your daughter's] giving you all that you need to fulfill your destiny. And may he express through you all that is excellent and pleasing to him through your life-union with Jesus the Anointed One who is to receive all glory forever! Amen!" Hebrews 13:21 (TPT)

Jentezen Franklin states in his book *Love Like You've Never Been Hurt* 2018, "Friend, your destiny is greater than your difficulty. Your destiny is greater than your disaster. Your destiny is greater than your present dilemma. Your destiny is greater than your fears."

Fear can lead to bad choices, and bad choices lead to bad outcomes. Like so many teen and preteen young girls, they oftentimes make bad decisions due to their lack of maturity, lack of self-worth, lack of wisdom, lack of having God's Word in their hearts, lack of an appropriate peer group, lack of proper parental guidance, numerous reasons, many of which they themselves do not understand. One encouraging scripture that we can instill in our daughters and speak over them is Jeremiah 29:11 (NIV), "For I know the plans I have for you," declared the Lord, "plans to prosper you and not to harm you, plans to give you hope and a future."

The Message reads, "I know what I'm doing. I have it all planned out- plans to take care of you, not abandon you, plans to give you the future you hope for. When you call me, when you come and pray to me, I'll listen. When you come looking for me, you'll find me. Yes, when you get serious about finding me and want it more than anything else, I'll make sure you won't be disappointed."

Parents always want the best for their children, and we grieve when our children make senseless mistakes; this is why instructing our daughters about pursuing their destiny is of the utmost importance. Our daughters need to know that they were born for a purpose here on earth and that every step they take and every choice they make, moves them one step closer to or one step farther away from their destiny. In Proverbs 5:23 (TPT), God warns us that, "Those who choose wickedness die for lack of self-control, for their foolish ways lead them astray, carrying them away as hostages-kidnapped captives robbed of destiny."

I don't want my daughters robbed of their destiny! Here are a few more scriptures that warn our daughters to be vigilant and aware:

O foolish Galatians! Who has bewitched you that you should not obey the truth...? Galatians 3:1 (NKJV)

Romans 16:17-19 (NIV) I urge you, brothers and sisters, to watch out for those who cause division and put obstacles in your way that are contrary to the teaching you have learned. Keep away from them. For such people are not serving our Lord Christ, but their own appetites. By smooth talk and flattery they deceive the minds of naïve people but I want you to be wise about what is good, and innocent about what is evil.

But unless a person repents, asks for forgiveness, and pursues restoration with the Lord, they cannot be restored and placed back on the right path for their life. We cannot let anything, or anyone hinder our daughters from earnestly seeking the Lord and His wisdom, and following the path set before them.

Spiritual Gifts

Therefore I remind you to stir up the gift of God which is in you through the laying on my hands. For God has

not given us a spirit of fear, but of power and of love
and of a sound mind.

2 Timothy 1:6-7 (NKJV)

The gift of God inside of you is important to share with others!
Someone needs your gift! --Unknown

Many years ago, I took a Spiritual Gifts Inventory and I learned that
my spiritual gift is prophecy. I do not call myself a prophet, but I have
been known to speak words of insight and wisdom to fellow believers.
I tend to view the world in black and white, with very few gray areas.
I tend to lack compassion for others, and I often have the desire to tell
others "How the cow ate the cabbage," which tends to come off as
offensive and abrasive.

I have unintentionally rubbed people the wrong way. This is
another reason why I questioned God about my personality. I did some
research and learned the prophets were not well liked; actually, they
were despised, persecuted, and even killed. Ouch!

Prophets were called by God and filled with God's Spirit to be
the mouthpiece to His people when they strayed from His Word and
began worshiping idols. When God's people became embroiled in sin,
He would send a prophet to warn them. These warnings often involved
punishment and consequences for their sins.

God has also gifted me with a love for writing and speaking His
truth, this is why I incorporate scriptures into my writings. In high
school, I had three of the best English teachers in the state of Texas:
Maureen Vurlicer, Doris Crisp, and Jane Smith; all three of them
prepared me for future writing assignments in college. I breezed through
Freshman Writing and was dumbfounded when I met students who had
never had any kind of formal writing instruction of any type; most
of them didn't know the difference between expository, persuasive,
research, or other forms of writing.

While at Texas A&M, I once wrote a letter to the editor of *The
Battalion*, A&M's student newspaper, expressing my opinion and disdain

regarding an offensive and tacky, irreverent t-shirt some girl in one of my classes was wearing. (Ask me about that one later). I doubt anyone read "my letter to the editor" and I don't remember anyone responding to it, but of course, I had to express my opinion.

I'm known for expressing my opinion, fervently, passionately, and often loudly, whether solicited or not. My opinions were and still are based largely on my beliefs, stemming from a Southern Baptist Christian upbringing. I knew all about Adam and Eve, and the Fall of Man, Noah, Jonah, Moses, the Ten Commandments, and most importantly, Jesus! Jesus was the Son of God, born of a virgin, crucified on a cross, and rose again on the third day to save us from our sins. I was never arrogant enough to think that my opinion was the only correct one, because it is in fact, an opinion, and everybody's got one. But I was secure enough in my Christian beliefs that I would debate with others about the *rights and wrongs* of the world.

After college I moved back home and in my spare time, nine months without a job or job prospects, I wrote several letters to the editor of my hometown newspaper. Not that I really thought other people would be interested in *my* opinions, but whenever I became aware of perplexing situations within the community, ones that were ethically or morally questionable, I wanted someone to rectify the situation; right the wrong. Not that I wanted to do anything about it myself, I wasn't a crusader or lobbyist, but I wanted someone to know there was a problem that needed to be remedied. I hoped that someone would reply to my letters with feasible solutions.

Some of the topics I covered in my letters were: prison inmates should not receive Pell Grants, children should not stand at busy intersections fundraising, Why does Port Arthur host a Janis Joplin Birthday Bash every year when it's known she detested our town?, and Why should I have to wait in line behind a lottery addict at the convenient store, just to pay for my gas? (I have copies of these letters if anyone is interested).

I was surprised when several people responded to my first "Letter to the Editor." Most people agreed with me, it seemed unfair to give Pell Grants to prison inmates when many law-abiding citizens yearned to go to college but could not afford to do so. And many people agreed with me, young children should not stand at busy intersections fundraising or collecting money for organizations such as Little League, marching band, or other extracurricular activities, without visible identification of affiliation with the organization; we also agreed that even with adult supervision it was dangerous.

To my surprise, after the letter regarding Lottery tickets was published, one of the responders personally addressed me as "Queen Stephanie" which I found rather funny because my name means "Crowned One." So, when I wrote the fourth letter about the Janis Joplin Birthday Bash, I addressed the readers as "My Loyal Subjects," and signed off with "Queen Stephanie." Sorry ladies, I can be a bit cheeky at times.

I'm still trying to figure out Sarah and Sophie's spiritual gifts, some have become a little more evident in the past year. Sarah has a big tender heart and wants to help people, so service may be her gift. Sophie's gift is exhortation; she is a cheerleader to everyone she meets, always encouraging them and rooting them on to do their best. In time as they grow and mature, not only physically but spiritually, their true giftings will present themselves. At that time, together we can work on cultivating those gifts as they make decisions regarding their future activities, education, vocations, and other important milestones.

Redemption

God always offers redemption to those of us who have strayed from His chosen path. If you are one of the wise and obedient ones, then you deserve a gold medal, but some of us took our lives into our own hands and screwed things up *royally*.

Fortunately, God is a loving and forgiving God, and He alone can straighten up and fix the huge messes that we make of our lives. Some of our messes are bigger than others, but I'm not judging, and as my former pastor used to say, "You better clean up your own backyard before you go criticizing your neighbor's backyard!"

God can and will redeem any and every situation that you've made a mess of, but we have to remember one thing, "You are free to choose, but you are not free from the consequences of your choice," Ezra Taft Benson. We cannot rationalize or defend our bad choices and bad behavior; the devil did not make you do it! True repentance is at the heart of true redemption; we need to realize that our waywardness and disobedience separates us from God, and only through the blood of Jesus Christ and the love of God, in addition to a true repentant heart, can our lives be redeemed. No one is a lost cause, "For no one is cast off by the Lord forever" Lamentations 3:31 (NIV). No one is beyond God's forgiveness and reach. We "all fall short of the glory of God" Romans 3:23 (NIV), but God's mercies "are new every morning" Lamentations 3:23 (KJV).

Oh, you can bet Satan will make every effort to derail your daughters from their God-chosen path to fulfilling their destiny. As society crumbles under the repercussions of sin, social morals falter, and lukewarm Christians fall away from the church and the truth of God's Word, we are left in a world of chaos and utter confusion, and we need to make sure our daughters aren't ignorant of His Word. How thankful we should be to God who loved us so, that He gave us His Word and has forewarned us of what is to come. In 2 Timothy 3:1-15, God plainly explains the chaos in today's world:

> But you need to be aware that in the final days the culture of society will become extremely fierce. People will be self-centered lovers of themselves and obsessed with money. They will boast of great things as they strut around in their arrogant pride and mock all that is

right. They will ignore their own families. They will be ungrateful and ungodly. They will become addicted to hateful and malicious slander. Slaves to their desires, they will be ferocious, belligerent haters of what is good and right. With brutal treachery, they will act without restraint, bigoted and wrapped in clouds of their conceit. They will find their delight in the pleasures of this world more than the pleasures of the loving God.

They may pretend to have respect for God, but in reality, they want nothing to do with God's power. Stay away from people like these! For they are the ones who worm their way into the hearts of vulnerable women, spending the night with those who are captured by their lusts and steeped in sin. They are always learning but never discover the revelation-knowledge of truth…. So it will be in the last days with those who reject the faith with their corrupt minds and arrogant hearts, standing against the truth of God. (The Passion Translation)

My purpose in sharing this passage of scripture is not to scare you or your daughters into fearful obedience, it is to inform them of what the future holds as we move closer to the coming of Christ. We all need to be ready and prepared because life as we know it is continually changing, and our daughters need to be prepared with total God confidence to withstand the trials that may come their way.

Let me remind you again, even if you've strayed from the path God has chosen for you, He will lead you back. No decision is final, except death. "Jesus has the last word on everything and everyone, from angels to armies. He's standing right alongside God, and what He says goes" 1 Peter 3:22 (MSG). Even Job in all of his suffering and loss knew, "You [the Lord] can do all things; no purpose of Yours can be thwarted" Job 42:2 (NIV). God's plans will come to fulfillment, whether anyone else likes it or not. Isaiah the prophet proclaimed in chapter 14:27 (NIV),

"For the Lord almighty has purposed, and who can thwart Him?" (NIV) No one will be able to stand between you and your daughter's God-given destiny.

I'd like to mention several other young women who in spite of tremendous obstacles and regardless of what "society" said they could or could not do, pursued their dreams, and have achieved or continue to achieve success. It's a good thing these brave women didn't listen to the nay-sayers, or we wouldn't be encouraged and blessed by their examples.

Brittney Spencer, a young rising star in country music, from Baltimore, Maryland who doesn't exactly fit the mold in the country music genre because she is African American. She doesn't look like your typical country music singer, but that hasn't stopped her from pursuing her passion. She was recently invited to sing at the Grand Ole Opry and has a chart-topping album that she worked on for eight years titled *Sober and Skinny*.

Amy Bockerstette is the first athlete with Down Syndrome to receive an athletic scholarship to attend college and the first to compete in a national golf collegiate championship. Amy is known for her "can do" attitude, and often reminds other competing players that, "I got this!", which also is the name of her foundation. On May 20, 2021, she made history when she competed in the 2021 NJCCA Women's Golf Championship held at Plantation Bay Golf & Country Club in Ormond Beach, Florida. A native of Arizona where she attends Paradise Valley Community College in Phoenix, she continues to play at the collegiate level while also pursuing a degree in dance.

Lizzy Howell, a talented young dancer from Delaware, courageously posted videos of herself on social media. I describe Lizzy as *courageous* because she doesn't have the "typical" dancer's body; she is a full-figured ballerina who was cyber bullied because she didn't fit the cookie-cutter shape of most ballerinas. She has endured teasing and ridicule most of her life because of her size. One instructor told her that she needed to lose weight, or she would never get a part in the Nutcracker. Dancing is Lizzy's passion and after her videos went viral with 20 million views, she realized that she was an encouragement to others who didn't fit the stereotypes for their passions, such as dance. Jordan Matter, a famous photographer, chose Lizzy to be in his book entitled *Born to Dance*. She has now been featured in *Teen Vogue*, *People*, and *Today*. Lizzy's determination to keep dancing has opened the doors to many opportunities including representing young women of all sizes in a Target commercial. Lizzy once stated, "I don't think my body type should limit my opportunities," and it hasn't, because she is walking, or should I say, dancing out her destiny.

Do not let anyone or anything get between you and your destiny!

Now may the God who brought us peace by raising from the dead our Lord Jesus Christ so that he will be the Great Shepherd of his flock; and by the power of the blood of the eternal covenant may he work perfection into every part of you giving you all that you need to fulfill your **destiny**. Hebrews 13:20-21 (TPT)

Before we were even born, he gave us our **destiny**; that we would fulfill the plan of God who always accomplishes every purpose and plan in his heart. Ephesians 1:11(b) (TPT)

MATES AND FRIENDS

A woman's heart should be so hidden in Christ, that a man should have to "seek Him first" to find her.

Marriage is difficult, it's hard, and it takes a lot of work to keep it going year, after year, after year. Committing to love, honor, and cherish someone for a lifetime sounds fairly easy before reality slaps you in the face, and the first fight between you and your spouse is over something mundane such as leaving dirty dishes in the sink. What? I didn't know that was a crime. It is true, opposites attract, i.e. Brad and Stephanie Arceneaux. My husband and I are polar opposites in every way you can imagine, except for three areas: our Christian beliefs and values, our unexpected mutual love of heavy metal music, and politics. Trying to decide where to eat dinner is a monumental and frustrating task; he loves Chinese food, seafood, and crawfish. Yuck! I love quiche, salads, and any kind of gourmet foods, which are difficult to come by in southeast Texas. We have a Mexican food restaurant on every corner, and just as many unhealthy fast-food joints on every other corner. So compromising is what we do, oftentimes with resignation in our hearts, accompanied by gritted teeth, eye rolling, and a huge sigh. But we make it work.

My desire is to see Sarah and Sophie find their perfect God-chosen mate to spend their lives with. I love the quote, "A man who will lead you to God and not to sin, is always worth the wait!" If you've read my first book, *WAIT Is a Four-Letter Word*, you know my struggle with waiting on the Lord for a husband; actually, waiting on Brad to get a clue. The path I chose as a young twentysomething didn't go as I had planned; it led to a failed marriage, divorce, two years of painfully growing spiritually, and then God sent me "the one", my husband Brad.

Our story is long and complicated, so I'll summarize *WAIT* for you. In short, I married the wrong man and was miserable, so we divorced and I was devastated. It took Jesus to redeem the mess I had made of my life and turn it into an amazing love story, not only my love story with Brad, but my love story with Jesus. I had to go back to *my first love*, so He could lead me to *my forever love*. Nineteen years of marriage, cancer, infertility, premature identical-twin daughters, and just recently a recurrence of cancer has been our journey, but we're still here testifying to God's goodness every day.

I cannot imagine the devastation it would cause our precious daughters, if Brad and I were to divorce. Their little trusting hearts would be crushed, and their still developing minds wouldn't understand. I cannot, I will not, do that to my children; and don't you be so sure that the thought has not crossed my mind, because it has. But my commitment is first and foremost to the Lord, and secondly, to Brad. Praise the Lord, as I grow spiritually and mature, and allow God to mold me, I'm slowly becoming the wife Brad needs, and the mother Sarah and Sophie deserve.

Our girls do not know our story because they are too young, but when they're old enough and mature enough, we'll share it with them. One of my deepest regrets is having a divorce *on my record*. I ardently pray that neither one of my girls will ever have to experience the heartbreak of divorce, so by sharing our story we hope they will garner from our experiences wisdom to make better choices.

While at Texas A&M, I attended many activities at the Baptist Student Union; the ministry offered lunch on Fridays along with a short sermon by the director, Monday night Care Groups, and other social outings. As a freshman, I met a sweet young lady named Shannon, who invited me to Monday Night Care Groups; I was excited for the chance to meet people who were like minded about our faith. Care Groups encompassed Bible study, new-found friendships, and a necessary Christian support network for many students who were far away from home and missed the comforts of their families.

Shannon was a Junior and was much more mature than I, regarding my walk with the Lord. She guided our group through many studies of the scriptures, kindly offered to pray with us if we were experiencing struggles or difficulties and made herself available to us by phone or in person, whenever we needed a friend. Shannon's heart was truly focused on the Lord and ministering to others.

Shannon also had a serious boyfriend at the time, and she talked about him a lot, by the end of that year they were engaged to be married. I was happy for Shannon, but also envious, because she had what all young college girls long for, a *Prince Charming*. Shannon had found her God-given soulmate, and her future seemed bright and full of exciting plans and adventures. Shannon shared with me a copy of the following poem, "Satisfaction." I taped it to the wall next to my bed, and every year when I moved to a new apartment or to the sorority house my senior year, I kept this poem with me to remind me that God had a perfect mate for me, and in time, my heart's desire would be satisfied. After doing some research, I found the poem "Satisfaction" under a different title, "Be Satisfied with Me."

Be Satisfied with Me

Everyone longs to give themselves to someone, to have a deep soul relationship with another, to be loved thoroughly and exclusively. But God wants a Christian to wait until he/she is satisfied, fulfilled, and content with being loved by Him alone. God wants a Christian to discover that only in Him can your satisfaction be found, then you will be capable of the perfect human relationship that God has planned for him/her. You will never be united with another until you are united with God; exclusive of anyone or anything else, exclusive of any other desires or longings. The Lord wants you to stop planning – stop wishing; and allow Him to give you the most thrilling exciting plan that you can imagine. Almighty God wants you to have the best! Please allow Him to give it to you. Just keep watching God, expecting the greatest things. Keep experiencing the satisfaction that He is the great *I am*! Don't worry. Don't look at the things others have gotten or that God has given to them. Don't look at the things you think you want. You just keep looking off and way up to our Lord or you'll miss what He wants to show you. And when you are ready, He will surprise you with a love far more wonderful than anyone would ever dream of. You see, until you are ready, and until the one God has for you is ready, until you are both satisfied with Him and the life He has prepared for you, you will not be able to experience the love that exemplifies your relationship with Abba Father, and this is the perfect love. And dear one, God wants you to have this wonderful love. He wants you to see in the flesh a picture of your everlasting union of beauty, perfection, and love that He offers you with Himself. Know that He loves you utterly. He is the great I AM. He is GOD. Believe and be satisfied.

—St. Anthony of Padua

1195 – 1231

Looking back, I wish I would have taken those words in that poem to heart believing God had a *Prince Charming* for me too, but one that wouldn't take too long to get here. Unfortunately, once I graduated from Texas A&M and moved back home with a seemingly useless degree in psychology, having no job, no job prospects, and certainly no prospective suitors, I kind of lost my way for a few years. But one thing I knew about myself was that "I'd rather be by myself, than be miserable in a relationship, just to have that companionship"; I liked myself more than I liked most people, so being alone didn't bother me, until it *did* bother me.

During a candid conversation with a good "friend" of mine, she asked my opinion about a situation she had been pondering. She'd been dating this guy for about a year, and they were talking about moving in together; that's just not something I would have ever considered doing. She explained that they had talked about marriage, but he hadn't yet proposed, so they were considering moving in together to save money. She felt they were wasting their money paying two rents, two electric bills, and two cable bills; she thought it just made sense and she really wanted to be with this guy.

So, I opened my big mouth, stated that, "She was only trying to justify her actions," and put my bigger foot into my big mouth. This was the season before true spiritual maturity had taken place, when "speaking the truth" was what I did, but I left out the most important part of the Bible's teachings. We are to "speak the truth *in love*" (Ephesian 4:15). Honestly, I didn't know how to do that.

My "friend" didn't receive my *judgmental* response well and retorted, "Well, aren't we being honest this evening?" I thought I'd always been honest with her, so why was this circumstance any different? She asked me for my opinion, and I gave her just that. She and I had been friends since high school and all throughout college; she knew me, she knew how I was raised, and she knew my beliefs. I also thought she knew that I loved her and our friendship meant the world to me, so I couldn't understand why she would be offended by my answer. I wasn't being judgmental, but she didn't see it that way. My response came from a deeply ingrained, deeply held belief system.

Needless to say, after that night I didn't hear from her again, until six months later when she and her boyfriend broke up, and she moved back home with her parents. I realized that my "friend" wanted *me* to say what *she* wanted to hear. She wanted me to agree with her in the decision she was leaning toward. Eventually, they got back together, she got pregnant, they got married, and as of today, are still together; I guess he really was a good guy. I was grieved by the dissolution of our friendship, and I missed her terribly, but the choice was not mine, it was hers. I wish we could have "agreed to disagree", but it wasn't meant to be.

My "friend" is fortunate, her story has a happy ending, but oftentimes, young, vulnerable, needy girls, get themselves into situations because they lack patience, self-esteem, a stable family home, or other variables that push them toward making questionable decisions that will have unknown but potentially life-long consequences. Realistically, many couples that live together rarely get married. I see the situation as a lack of commitment on one or both person's part. I can't imagine setting up a household with someone without a commitment, a marriage, no, actually a covenant; I don't think I would have much faith in the security of the relationship, but that's just me. Please understand, I'm not being judgmental, I personally feel that there's a better way, God's way, and this is what I want for my girls. The world says it's okay to live with a person before you marry them, but we all know what that leads to. Make your own inferences, but what does the Bible say about this? Don't take my word for it, read the Word, search for the answers to your questions, and find the truth in His Word and what He desires for you and for your daughters.

I'm ending this section with an extremely sad, but true quote by Jerry Flowers:

The dangerous thing about acting like his wife, is after the rehearsal, you may not even get the part.

God-Given Friends

Have you heard the saying, "You are the peanut butter to my jelly?" Such an endearing sentiment about a close, cherished friend; a confidant, a sounding board, someone that you can be completely vulnerable and honest with, and they still love and accept you. God has blessed me with a small circle of dearly loved friends; each one completely different from the other, and each fills a different need in my heart.

You've already met Angie, we've known each other for twenty years, we live in the same city, we attend the same church, and our daughters are best friends. Happily, we get to see each other frequently. She is my coffee cohort and constant companion.

Ginger is my soul sister; we met fifteen years ago in a small couples' group at church. We are both prophetic and understand each other completely. When we talk, we're always on the same spiritual wavelength. We love many of the same things: fashion, jewelry, handbags. I once called her my *shopping twin*. We both love expensive but probably *not in our budget* merchandise and The Galleria is our Shopping Wonderland. Oftentimes we joke that our husbands don't appreciate their "arm candy." Ginger moved away about ten years ago, but we talk on the phone frequently and I get to see her two to three times a year when she flies down to visit her parents.

Then there's Amy and Rondell; they are the "B" and "L", to my "T". Get it? B-L-T. I'd rather be the "L", but Rondell hates tomatoes, so I have to be the "T". Amy is the "B" because she loves bacon. Amy is our "calm in the storm," she is rational, reasonable, gives great advice, and her spiritual gift is exhortation. Rondell is the "L", she is constantly learning, a braniac, a seeker of information, our tour guide on every trip we take, but she does have an addiction to Google Maps; her phone is surgically attached to her hand. I am the "T", the glue that holds us all together, the truth teller, the quoter of scriptures, and probably the most talkative of our group. We all speak our minds, but I probably speak my opinion the loudest. I have known Rondell since I was in the fourth grade, and I met Amy in middle school. All three of us attended the same middle and high schools and have been the greatest of friends. We were bridesmaids in each other's weddings and watched each other's children grow up. We all live in Texas, but hundreds of miles away from each other. We don't get to see or talk to each other as often as we'd like, but we do try.

About seven years ago, we decided to seriously make an effort to see each other more, so began our yearly girls' trip. We've been on a cruise to Cozumel and swam with the dolphins, to New York City, 911 Memorial, and a Broadway musical, an air boating tour through the swamps of New Orleans, Fredericksburg Market Days, zip lining in Wimberley, horseback riding in Blanco, and all over the Texas Hill Country.

So far, Sarah and Sophie have been blessed with many friends from church. We have a group of seven little girls all born within a year of each other. They've grown up together, attended numerous church functions together, birthday parties, Christmas parties and sleepovers. The bonds created through their shared Christian upbringing have established friendships that will hopefully last forever.

We also have a street full of kids affectionately known as "The Memphis Street Mafia," Memphis being the name of our street. The nomenclature might be somewhat misleading because they are all really good kids. We have ten kids from four families who have become great friends through the years: there are two sets of identical twin girls, two girls named Reese, and the girls outnumber the boys eight to two. We've had crawfish boils, fish fries, birthday parties, and celebrated other holidays with tons of food. We absolutely love our neighbors and their kids. The best aspect of our neighborhood is we often congregate on one another's driveway to visit, while our kids play until the sun goes down. They ride their hoverboards, bikes, electric cars, scooters, play baseball, basketball, jump on our trampoline, and climb the tree in our front yard. What a picturesque memory to behold, one that is rarely seen these days.

I hope I don't sound naïve when I speak about my hopes and dreams for my daughters' lives, I know that strong faith and spiritual growth come only from being tested. Adversity is how we grow our faith. As a mother, I want to shield and protect Sarah and Sophie from hurt, disappointment, or heartbreak, but I know the truth is "the testing of our faith produces endurance (patience), and endurance produces character" Romans 5:3-4 (ESV). "Consider it a great joy, my brothers and sisters, whenever you experience various trials, because you know that the testing of your faith produces endurance. And let endurance have its full effect, so that you [my daughters] may be mature and complete, lacking nothing" James 1:2-4 (CSB). Letting go and letting God guide the narrative of their lives will take faith and trust on my part, but I know He's got this!

13

THE ULTIMATE DECEPTION

Therefore, there is now no condemnation for those who
are in Christ Jesus. Romans 8:1 (NIV)

Truth is not relative. The only truth we have is God's Word, and His
Word is absolute. We've been hearing for the past few years about
people "telling their truth." There is no such thing as "your truth" or
"my truth" because our truths are subjective. Granted, when you and
I are having a conversation, I hope that the words you are speaking to
me are the truth, meaning I hope you are not lying to me or deceiving
me in any way. I hope that we can be honest with each other in our
verbal interactions, having the assurance that we are honorable and
forthcoming (forthright) with each other, so as to maintain the integrity
of our relationship (friendship).

The problem with the concept of "my truth" is that we are sinful
creatures, and our truth is subjective because every word that we speak
is tainted by sin. Our truth is based upon the sum of our life experiences,
which include our thoughts and beliefs. Many of our life experiences
may be similar, but not exactly the same. No two people have the exact

experience, not even my identical twin daughters will have identical experiences, and they share the exact same DNA.

Perception is a neurophysiological process, including memory, by which an organism becomes aware of and interprets external stimuli; a way of regarding, understanding, or interpreting something.

Example: If "your truth" is that your mother abandoned you as a child, your reaction to this circumstance will be perceived differently than by other people depending on how one was raised, how much love and support one received while growing up, your belief that God can turn "ashes to beauty" and God will take "what Satan meant for harm and turn it into good." Perception is the lens through which we view the world. Your world needs to be framed by God's Word because his Word is truth. If you need to refresh your memory, go back and review the chapter on "God's Word Is Truth."

My daughters have a close friend named Cadence. Cadence's mom, Angie, and I have been friends for twenty years. We were both "late bloomers" and had our children later in life; Sarah, Sophie, and Cadence really had no choice in becoming friends because Angie and I already had a long standing friendship. Both of us were excited when our girls were born only six weeks apart. As the girls have grown, they have spent lots of time together; playdates, swimming lessons, birthday parties, VBS, and baking camp have filled their lives with activities and companionship. They truly are more like siblings than friends.

Nine years have come and gone in the blink of an eye, and Cadence still cannot tell the difference between Sarah and Sophie. Their obvious differences have only become evident in the past few years as their personalities, which are completely different, have emerged and developed. Sarah is our princess with long flowing brown hair with natural red and blond streaks. She's foo-foo-y, loves dresses, high heels, jewelry, and handbags. Sophie on the other hand is our athlete; some would call her our "tomboy." Sophie really does not like the term "tomboy" and when she voiced her dislike of the term, we changed our terminology to "tomgirl" because it accurately relates the message that, yes in fact, she is a girl, even if she doesn't share her sister's love of pink, frilly dresses, hoochie mama shoes, and tiaras. Sophie prefers the color blue, athleisure wear, jeans and sneakers, baseball caps and physically strenuous sports like jiu jitsu, soccer, and wrestling with her friend Ryder, who secretly has a crush on her and has had a crush on her since they were about three years old.

Many people ask me, "How do you tell them apart?" Well, I'm their mom and I know my own children. Because everyone else has difficulty telling them apart, I usually explain, Sarah = princess, Sophie = athlete. Now that they dress differently and have different hair styles, it is much easier for people to tell them apart. Fortunately for Cadence, Sarah likes to wear her hair really long, like to her waist-long and Sophie now prefers her hair cut shorter, right above her shoulders. The identity problem for friends and family has been solved. Sarah = long hair and Sophie = short hair. You're welcome.

It's funny that through the years when Cadence would tattle tell on one of my girls, I'd ask which one she was talking about and she'd say, "that one," while pointing her finger at one of them. She truly couldn't tell them apart.

Angie related to me a conversation she had with Cadence about my girls. Cadence has heard me, as well as her mom, trying to explain the differences between Sarah and Sophie to others at church, at parties, or out in public. The term "tomboy" comes up quite often. One day Cadence asked Angie, "Now, which one is the boy?" Angie corrected her and said, "Sophie is not a boy, honey, people sometimes refer to her as a "tomboy", but she is 100% a girl." Thankfully, Angie took the time to explain the verbiage "tomboy" to Cadence to help in her understanding.

Young children are so innocent, vulnerable, and impressionable; if they don't have someone in their lives to explain their world to them, they might possibly be confused or misinformed. Children are trusting and believe pretty much anything you tell them, i.e., Santa brings gifts on Christmas Eve, the Tooth Fairy leaves money for lost teeth, or the Easter Bunny delivers chocolates and Easter eggs. Christian parents have a responsibility to raise their children knowing the truth about their personhood, their identity. Looks can be deceiving, but God has given us one foolproof way of determining whether our children are boys or girls; their DNA. Our DNA is infallible. It determines everything about us – our gender, our race, the color of our hair, skin, and eyes, our height and optimal weight, I.Q., and thousands of other characteristics about us. DNA cannot lie.

So, the controversial debate about gender identity is easily solved by evaluating one's DNA. Scientists who have studied DNA (Watson and Crick) discovered that our sex chromosomes determine whether we are a boy (XY) or a girl (XX). Biological males carry both sex chromosomes in their DNA. Biological females only carry one sex chromosome in their DNA; this is the reason men are the ones who contribute the DNA that determines the sex of a baby.

God is the author of life. He is the creator of DNA and when God forms a baby in his/her mother's womb, He knows exactly who He is creating; a unique human being in the likeness and image of Himself. Since the beginning of time, humans have been created in God's image, as Genesis 1:27 (NIV) states, "So God created mankind in His *own* image; in the image of God, He created them; male and female He created them. God blessed them, and said to them, 'Be fruitful and multiply.'"

What is gender? Webster's dictionary defines gender as the behavioral, cultural, or psychological traits typically associated with one sex.

What is sex? Webster's dictionary defines sex as either of the two major forms of individuals that occur in many species and that are distinguished respectively as female or male especially on the basis of their reproductive organs and structures.

What is gender identity? The first known use of the term "gender identity" was in 1964. A person's internal sense of being male, female, some combination of male and female, or neither male nor female. Here is an example: Those seeking state driver's licenses in Massachusetts are closer to being able to designate their gender as "X" instead of "male" or "female." The state Senate has overwhelmingly approved a bill that would allow for the nonbinary designation on licenses. –Steve LeBlanc. Why would anyone want to be identified as an "X"; it's so impersonal and vague?

Here is another example: Facebook's message was clear when the social media network added new gender options for users on Thursday; the company is sensitive to a wide spectrum of gender identity and wants users to feel accommodated no matter where they see themselves on that spectrum. – Katy Steinmetz

Facebook provides more than fifty options beyond "male" and "female" for users to describe their gender identity, from "gender questioning" and "neither" to "androgynous". –The Chicago Times. This is another example of the largest social platform in the world, perpetuating the ambiguity of gender.

God's timing is so perfect. I was fortunate to share my pregnancy experience with my good friend, Angie, who got pregnant about two months before I did. We have been friends for twenty years, so we share a long history. Although it took ten years for Brad and I to conceive, I was somewhat scared to face this parenting adventure all by myself. I was excited to be able to share in the joy of such an amazing adventure with my friend.

As our girls got older, our schedules were filled with playdates and greatly needed outings; Angie and I would discuss every topic under the sun regarding our growing babies. Their sleep patterns, doctors' visits, food preferences, potty training, putting them in the nursery every Sunday for a necessary break, and how fascinating it was to watch their individual personalities develop. Although Sarah and Sophie are identical twins, it was obvious from about the age of eight months or so, the differences in their personalities began to emerge.

For the first few years, we felt we were drowning in our responsibilities as parents. Parenting is hard, extremely hard, and I had two babies to take care of and I felt overwhelmed and exhausted most of the time. Angie only has one child, but she was working full time, in a new job and she was burning the candle at both ends. I feel having children later on in life presents issues that younger mothers may not deal with, lack of energy! Fortunately, I was blessed to have my parents and my mother-in-law's help for the first eighteen months of Sarah and Sophie's lives.

Our conversation centered around our hopes and dreams for our daughters. Like most mothers, we wanted our little girls to be healthy, happy, smart, creative, and follow their dreams. I jotted down a list of topics that I could begin praying about. These topics prompted many hours of discussions between Angie and I. We even discussed our desire for Godly Christians husbands for our girls. I specifically wanted my girls to know at a young age what they were passionate about, and to pursue those passions. I wanted their passions to evolve into careers that they loved and could generate income to take care of themselves. Most importantly, we both wanted for our daughters to walk in the path that God had chosen for them and to fulfill their destinies.

We discussed these important matters over a hot cup of coffee and sometimes a needed dessert; these therapy sessions calmed my anxious thoughts and helped me feel I had a kindred spirit, a sounding board, and not so alone in the daily struggles of Mommie-hood. These areas of concern filled my thoughts at night, and I would talk with God about them; you are probably thinking, "Ok lady, aren't you getting a little ahead of yourself?" I know, it might seem a bit premature for the mother of six-month-old twins to start contemplating their futures, but I wanted to be prepared and wanted my daughters to be prepared for whatever may come their way.

One area of concern that kept bombarding my thoughts was the notion that Sarah and Sophie could be deceived in their thinking, in their minds. I believe this concern stemmed from what I was seeing on television, social media, in schools, in public spaces, and hearing on the radio: the rising tendency toward transgenderism, a concept I could not wrap my head around. I just could not understand why a beloved little girl, teenager, or adult woman whom God had created, would choose to disavow her God-given gender, and choose to become a boy. This perplexing social issue had my emotions in knots. I'm not one to worry, but I am one to ponder such things, so, I began praying each night and asking the Lord to protect Sarah and Sophie's precious little innocent minds from lying thoughts, and "that they would *never* be deceived in their thinking."

The reason I felt the need to address the issues of transgenderism and gender identity in this book is because our daughters are being deceived. Being deceived begins in your mind with your thoughts. 2 Corinthians 11:3-4 (TPT) tells us, "But now I'm afraid that just as Eve was deceived by the serpent's clever lies, your thoughts may be corrupted and you may lose your single-hearted devotion and pure love for Christ."

I do not want to give Satan any more attention than he deserves, but let me share with you several scriptures that describe exactly who he is, so that you don't take his presence in this world lightly. In John 8:44 (NIV) we learn, "He was a murderer from the beginning, not holding to the truth, for there is no truth in him. When he lies, he speaks his native language, for he is a liar and the father of lies." In Genesis 3:1 (AMP), "Now the serpent was more crafty (subtle, skilled in deceit) than any living creature of the field which the Lord God had made. And the serpent (Satan) said to the woman, 'Can it really be that God has said, 'You shall not eat from any tree of the garden?' And the woman said to the serpent, 'We may eat fruit from the trees of the garden, except the fruit from the tree which is in the middle of the garden.' God said, 'You shall not eat from it nor touch it, otherwise you will die.' But the serpent said to the woman, 'You certainly will not die!'" As the story goes, Eve ate of the forbidden fruit and so did Adam, and thus "the Fall of Man." Who did Eve believe? She had two choices, God or Satan, and she chose to believe Satan. "For our struggle is not against flesh and blood, but against the rulers, against the authorities, against the powers of this dark world and against spiritual forces of evil in the heavenly realms" Ephesians 6:12 (NIV). Who will our daughters believe, God and His Holy Word, or Satan and his lies? He deceived Eve, and he wants to deceive our daughters.

We discussed in the chapter "God's Word Is Truth," how important it is to have the Word of God securely planted in our daughters' hearts. In Psalm 119:11, King David says to God, "I have hidden your word in my heart that I might not sin against you." This is a purposeful decision that requires action.

Many young women today are facing a crisis of identity. Satan uses thoughts to deceive us. We are bombarded daily with thoughts, and we have to recognize who or where those thoughts are coming from. I know that if my thoughts are encouraging and positive, they must have come from the Lord, but if my thoughts are negative, disparaging, or depressing, I know that they come from Satan. I'd like to use the analogy of a seed to explain how deceptive thoughts take hold in our minds. A thought (a lie) like a seed can be planted into the mind of a person. For example, "I'm not smart, I'm unlovable, I'm broken." If we do not have the Word of God [the truth] ever before us, we are susceptible to believing the lie. Such lies begin to take root in our minds when we intentionally or unintentionally begin to dwell or ponder the thought [the lie]. Unfortunately, we encounter people or circumstances that tend to reinforce those thoughts, "I'm not smart, I'm unlovable, I'm broken." The more we rehearse the lie, the more it becomes ingrained into our thinking. Every time we think about it, question it, talk about it, the lie is being "watered" and like a seed it eventually takes root and engulfs the mind leading some to surrender to that lie, which sadly becomes "their truth."

Our minds are the battlefield, and Satan will take full advantage of young girls who do not know the truth (God's Word) and who they are in Christ. This is why the scripture in 2 Corinthians 10:5b instructs us to "Cast down arguments and every lofty thing that exalts itself against the knowledge of God and bringing into captivity every thought to the obedience of Christ" (KJV 2000). If we have a thought that doesn't line up with the Word of God and Jesus' teachings, thoughts that blatantly contradict God's Word, then we need to cast it down and out of our minds.

"For though we walk in the flesh, we do not war after the flesh. For the weapons of our warfare are not carnal, but mighty through God to the pulling down of strongholds" 2 Corinthians 10:5a (KJV). We've discussed strongholds earlier in this book. Strongholds are first established in the mind; that is why we are to take every thought captive. Behind a stronghold is also a lie- a place of personal bondage where God's Word has been subjugated to an unscriptural idea or personally confused belief that is held to be true. (Kingdom Dynamics p. 1621)

Regarding the issue of transgenderism, I'd like to address the deceptive way that Satan perverts what God has created. He twists the thoughts of innocent children, engaging them in an ongoing battle to change who God has created them to be. God doesn't make mistakes, but Satan tries to make young children believe they were born into the wrong body. This is a treacherous lie. Jeremiah 29:11 (NIV) states, "For I know the plans I have for you", declares the Lord. "Plans to prosper you and not to harm you, plans to give you hope and a future." If young children are not immersed in the Word of God and what His Word says about them, their future, and His purpose for their lives, they can easily believe that God has made a mistake. However, when presented with the truth of God's Word in Jeremiah 29:11, the truth will be planted in their hearts, instead of a lie.

I'll use the example of a young girl who accidentally overhears her friends saying *she looks like a boy* because of her short haircut. Every child will react differently to those words. I had short hair when I was a young girl, and I didn't think that made me a boy. And I had parents who reinforced the fact that I was a girl. If I had said to my parents that I thought I was a boy (male), they would have responded with "That is nonsense", and then took the time to explain to me how God created girls and boys differently. My parents would never have encouraged or cultivated that lie. They would not have allowed me to dress like a boy, act like a boy, or anything else that was contrary to who I really was, and that is a girl (female).

However, many children are not raised in Christian homes with parents who will speak the truth to them and guide them with the truth of God's Word. Children cannot be left to raise themselves; they must be taught the precepts and commandments of God, and about Jesus' love and sacrifice for us. If a child is left to navigate this world alone without the wisdom from the Word and parameters for acceptable and non-acceptable behavior, they will be utterly lost. If a child is allowed to do as she pleases, dress like a boy when she is a girl, those thoughts that she has about herself, "I must be a boy because I have short hair, I'm not as feminine as other girls therefore I must be a boy, I don't wear makeup or dresses so I must me a boy," (whatever the deceptive thoughts may be) other people's acceptance of her *new identity* will be reinforced when she dresses like a boy, talks like a boy, acts like a boy, and as we hear the terminology today "identifies as a boy."

Children ages three to early teens do not have the higher order reasoning skills to make life changing decision about many things, especially their sex and who they are. They lack the ability to think abstractly about current behaviors and choices, and the future consequences of those choices.

The Bible exhorts us in Romans 12:2 (AMP), "And do not be conformed to this world [any longer with its superficial values and customs], but be transformed and progressively changed [as you mature spiritually] by the renewing of your mind [focusing on godly values and ethical attitudes], so that you may prove [for yourselves] what the will of God is, that which is good and acceptable and perfect [in His plan and purpose for you].

We have the ultimate handbook called the Bible, and we need to use it to address this issue of transgenderism. Look what this phenomenon is doing to our children; transgender children tend to be more depressed than other children, have higher rates of suicide, and their chosen lifestyle causes division in families and often destroys relationships. They are mutilating their bodies because they believe a lie. This is exactly what Satan does; he comes to kill, steal, and destroy.

Please hear my heart, Jesus' heart, I am not sitting in judgment of anyone, that is God's job and He is loving and just; He is the only one who can judge a man's heart. I began this chapter with the scripture from Romans 8:1, "Now there is no condemnation for those who are in Christ Jesus." My responsibility as a Believer is to "love thy neighbor as thyself" and to be the hands and feet of Jesus here on this earth. To share His message of love and forgiveness. His word promises that "Therefore, if anyone is in Christ, he [she] is a new creation; old things have passed away; behold, all things have become new" Corinthians 5:17 (NKJV).

Jesus loves you just the way you are, but he also loves you enough to show you the truth so you can be set free from stronghold, behaviors, attitudes, addictions, and lie, and so that you will "know the truth and the truth will set you free" John 8:32 (NIV).

My goal is to spread God's Word, His truth, to others. My heart truly aches for young women and men, who find themselves in situations or relationships that only bring pain, dissatisfaction, and disillusionment and whose families have been devastated by this accepted lie. I want everyone to know the truth because it will set them free.

I want to be the person who speaks truth into your life; the one who shares God's holy words with you, so that you will be set free from a lifestyle founded upon lies. I know that this is an extremely controversial subject, and many people won't even broach the topic because they fear being labeled a bigot, a hater, or discriminatory. I am none of those, I am only trying to shed the light of God's Word onto situations where people need it. "How sweet are Your words to my taste, sweeter than honey to my mouth! Through Your precepts I get understanding; Therefore I hate every false way. Your word *is* a lamp to my feet and a light unto my path" Psalms 119:103-105 (NKJV) . The Word of God makes what is confusing crystal clear.

Another controversial topic within our society is homosexuality and lesbianism. I majored in psychology (the scientific study of the human mind and its functions, especially those affecting behavior), while attending Texas A&M University. I have always been fascinated with human behavior and why people do what they do. What causes a person to behave in a certain way? What unseen forces are manipulating their actions and reactions? Why do some people interact appropriately with others, and yet some people are social misfits? Why do some people follow the rules and others rebel against the rules? In the process of completing my Bachelor of Science degree, I had many psychology course options: Abnormal Psychology (fascinating), Developmental Psychology (possibly took but I don't remember), Neuroscience, or Learning and Memory (I wasn't smart enough to take either one of those), but Human Sexuality piqued my curiosity, so for grins, I signed up for the course. About halfway through the semester, our professor announced that during our next scheduled class we would have a panel of guest who were all members of the Texas A&M Gay and Lesbian Society. Record scratch #2! Hold on, wait a minute; I didn't know that A&M had a Gay and Lesbian Society. I thought A&M was a conservative university. Okay, someone is going to have to explain this one to me. I shouldn't have been shocked, but I was because I lived in my own little bubble of naivety.

The panel consisted of three women and three men, all who were students in my class. Forgive me for offending anyone with my reaction to stereotypical assumptions on the appearance of said members of the panel, but my first thought was, "Some of them don't look gay." As I said, stereotypical images which I had seen on TV and in the movies did not quite conform with the reality of what my eyes beheld. Each student on the panel introduced themselves and shared their story with the class. The burning question in my mind was, "Why do they think they are gay? What happened to them during childhood that led them to believe they were gay?"

One of the women on the panel was dressed like a *sorority chick*, pretty, face and hair made up, gigantic bow in her hair; she looked like many of my sorority sisters. Ignorantly, I would have never known she was gay if she hadn't been a participant on the panel. Her story and her reasoning as to how she knew she was gay caused some cognitive dissonance for me. Cognitive dissonance is when we experience mental stress or discomfort because we hold two or more contradictory beliefs, ideas, or values at the same time. She explained that when she was about eight years old, she had a poster of Farrah Fawcett on her bedroom wall. She said that she loved Farrah Fawcett, that she was in-love with Farrah Fawcett; therefore, she knew she was gay.

Now hold up sister, when I was eight years old, I had a poster of Olivia Newton-John on my bedroom wall. I loved Olivia Newton-John, I was probably in-love with Olivia Newton-John but knowing how I felt about her did not cause me to think I was *gay*; I didn't even know what the term "gay" meant. I had a childhood crush on her; I admired her not only for her beauty, but for her amazing singing voice. I saw the movie *Grease* when it came to our local theater, and my aunt and uncle bought me the *Grease* double-record album for Christmas. I might have actually been obsessed with her. I can't tell you how many times I have watched the movie *Grease* throughout the years. And how many Saturday nights sleepovers were spent listening to the soundtrack over, and over, and over again. Of course, we always had singing competitions to decide who performed the best rendition of "Hopelessly Devoted to You" or "We Go Together." But it never crossed my mind that my childish, innocent feelings for her were wrong or misplaced, and I certainly was too young to contemplate whether my feelings were romantic or sexual in nature. I didn't even know what sex was at that age. The entire reasoning process seemed preposterous to me.

Most young children have an idol that they look up to, usually someone famous: athletes, singers, dancers, actors, You-Tubers, Tik-Tok-ers, video gamers, even teachers. Whether the idol is of the same sex or opposite sex as the child, is irrelevant because it's natural for children to admirer people who are famous or in the spotlight.

That eight-year-old girl, who now sat before me as a woman, had somehow misinterpreted her affectionate feelings toward Farrah Fawcett, for romantic feelings; that is why children need parents to guide them and help them sort out things that they don't understand.

This is when we need Scripture the most, to help frame our children's point of reference (the truth and authority of God's Word) regarding deceptive and destructive thoughts, wrong thinking, misleading ideals, ungodly belief systems that society holds, anything that is contradictory to God's Word. This is when knowing the truth is imperative to our daughters' success in interpreting, processing, and "casting down" the continual bombardment of lies from the enemy.

If your daughter is struggling with negative or lying thoughts, the Bible tells us, "For truth is a bright beam of light shining into every area of your life, instructing and correcting you to discover the ways of godly living" Proverbs 6:23 (TPT). Show her in the Word that God sees her. "She (Hagar) gave this name to the LORD who spoke to her: 'You are the God who sees me', for she said, 'I have now seen the One who sees me'" Genesis 16:13 (NIV). The truth points to the power of the gospel to redeem and to transform. "For I'm releasing these words to you this day, yes, even to you, so that your living hope will be found in God alone, for he is the only one who is always true" Proverbs 22:19. [Redemption] "Therefore, if anyone is in Christ, he is a new creation; old things have passed away; behold, all things have become new" 2 Corinthians 5:17. [Transformation]

And please remember what Jesus instructed us to do, "A new commandment I give to you, that you love one another; just as I have loved you, you are also to love one another. By this all people will know that you are my disciples, if you have love for one another." Please also remember, "It is the **goodness of God** that leads people to repentance," [not judgment, nor hate] Romans 2:4 (NKJV).

I love the quote by Jerry Bridges, "God's unfailing love for us is an objective fact affirmed over and over in the Scriptures. It is true whether we believe it or not. Our doubts do not destroy God's love, nor does our faith create it. It originates in the very nature of God, who is love, and it flows to us through our union with His beloved Son."

> But now, thus says the Lord, who created you, O Jacob [insert your name here], And He who formed you, O Israel; Fear not, for I have redeemed you; **I have called you by name, You are Mine**. Isaiah 43:1 (NKJV)

For more information on this topic, you can watch the movie *In His Image: Delighting in God's Plan for Gender and Sexuality* (2020) by American Family Studios.

CONCLUSION

The words that are penned in this book are the hopes and dreams I have for my daughters, and for all the daughters of the world. I have no control over their lives, but I know the One who does, so I place my trust in Him to guide and direct them on their individual paths. My hope is that Sarah and Sophie know deep down in their hearts how much God loves them, not by intellectual ascent, but real heart knowledge. My prayer for them is to "seek ye first the kingdom of God, and his righteousness; and all these things (passions, talents, relationships, education, spouse, children, and vocations) shall be added unto you" Matthew 6:33 (KJV).

I've told my story, I've tried to live what I believe, and my hope is that what I've shared in this book will minister to others because as Christians, one of our purposes is to share what God has done for us. I love the quote from my pastor, Andy Sink, "Live out loud and on purpose!" I pray the legacy I leave to Sarah and Sophie is filled with "love for God and His Word, love for others, gifts, talents, laughter, stories, intelligence, books, journals, smiles and helping hands." I believe the truth of God's Word written on these pages will inspire them to seek out their own personal relationship with Jesus, and to carry His truth into the next generation. Blessed mothers, I know you want the same for your beloved daughters.

I also want my girls to remember that beauty is only skin deep, and it fades with the passing of years; but "Three things will last forever-- faith, hope, and love-- and the greatest of these is love" 1 Corinthians 13:13 (NLT).

So daughters of God, believe His words and what He says about you; you are loved, you are precious in His sight, you are a chosen one, you are a beautiful masterpiece in the Creator's hands, you are known, you are wanted, you are sought after, you are heard, thought of, the apple of His eye, and the *one* He gave up His only begotten Son for, to save you from your sins and bring you into an amazing relationship with Himself.

Hide God's Word deep in your hearts. Know and believe that you are valued, and your worth comes only through a relationship with Him. Embrace your God given uniqueness. Lay hold of your divinely appointed destiny and remember to put on the full armor of God daily so that you may fight the good fight. And don't forget to put on your WARPAINT!

Printed in the United States
by Baker & Taylor Publisher Services